Islam and the Foundations of Political Power

In Translation: Modern Muslim Thinkers
Series Editor: Abdou Filali-Ansary

Books in the series include

*Islam:
Between Message and History*
Abdelmadjid Charfi

Islam and the Foundations of Political Power
Ali Abdel Razek

Governance from the Perspective of Islam
Ayatullah Aqa Sheikh Muhammad Hussein Na'ini
With a Commentary by
Ayatullah Sayyid Mahmud Taleqani

www.euppublishing.com/series/tmmt

Islam and the Foundations of Political Power

ALI ABDEL RAZEK

Translated by
Maryam Loutfi

Edited by
Abdou Filali-Ansary

EDINBURGH
University Press

IN ASSOCIATION WITH

THE AGA KHAN UNIVERSITY
INSTITUTE FOR THE STUDY OF MUSLIM CIVILISATIONS

The opinions expressed in this volume are those of the authors and do not necessarily reflect those of the Aga Khan University, Institute for the Study of Muslim Civilisations.

© Ali Abdel Razek, 1925
Introduction © Abdou Filali-Ansary, 2012, 2013
English translation © Aga Khan University, Institute for the Study of Muslim Civilisations, 2012, 2013

First published in hardback in 2012 by
Edinburgh University Press Ltd
22 George Square, Edinburgh EH8 9LF
www.euppublishing.com

This paperback edition 2013

Typeset in Garamond Premier
by Koinonia, Manchester, and
printed and bound in Great Britain
CPI Group (UK) Ltd, Croydon CR0 4YY

A CIP record for this book is available
from the British Library

ISBN 978 0 7486 3978 6 (hardback)
ISBN 978 0 7486 8983 5 (paperback)
ISBN 978 0 7486 5631 8 (webready PDF)
ISBN 978 0 7486 5633 2 (epub)

The right of Ali Abdel Razek and Abdou Filali-Ansary to be identified as authors of this work has been asserted in accordance with the Copyright, Designs and Patents Act 1988 and the Copyright and Related Rights Regulations 2003 (SI No. 2498).

Contents

About the Author   vi
A Tribute to Ali Abdel Razek from his Grandson, Amr Hamed   vii
Preface   xi

Introduction   1
Foreword   21

Book One: The Caliphate and Islam

1. The Nature of the Caliphate   25
2. The Status of the Caliphate   35
3. The Caliphate from the Social Point of View   43

Book Two: Islam and Government

4. The System of Power at the Time of the Prophet   59
5. Prophecy and Power   67
6. Islam: A Message from God rather than a System of Government; A Religion rather than a State   81

Book Three: The Caliphate and the Government throughout History

7. Religious Unity and the Arab People   99
8. The Arab State   107
9. The Nature of the Caliphate   111

List of Sources referred to by Abdel Razek   119
Appendix   123
Index   126

About the Author

Ali Abdel Razek was born in 1888 in Abu Jirj, middle Egypt, to a family of wealthy, politically active landowners. His father and brother were renowned as liberals, who opposed both the Wafd Nationalist Party that fought against British rule in Egypt and the conservatives, who were mostly allies of the monarchy. Abdel Razek was educated in the traditional Islamic curriculum and graduated from al-Azhar University as an 'alim[1] in 1915.

Following his graduation from al-Azhar, Abdel Razek received an introduction to modern university education, enrolling for courses at the newly founded Egyptian University. He also spent a few months at Oxford University, where he studied politics and economics; however, his time there was cut short with the outbreak of the First World War. He later became a teacher of Arabic and a judge (*qadi*) in the traditional Islamic courts of Alexandria.

It was during his time as a qadi that he began to investigate the founders of the Islamic justice system. He went on to examine the caliphate as the institution which lies at the root of the "Islamic" social order and of which the justice system is an instrument. It must be added here, that it was the overall context at the time that provided a pressing initiative for such reflections; especially with the abrogation of the caliphate and the angst it had created.

After being stripped of his title of 'alim and banned from any positions related to it, it is said that Abdel Razek immediately changed his external appearance, adopting European clothes and displaying a disregard for traditional style, habits and appearance.

Following the storm of criticism stirred by his essay, he made only a short return to public office (as minister of Islamic affairs). Abdel Razek eventually withdrew from the intellectual scene, took refuge in a stubborn silence and built himself a room in a tower where he dedicated the remainder of his life to study.

---

1 A traditional scholar or theologian.

A Tribute to Ali Abdel Razek from his Grandson, Amr Hamed

It was still dawn outside when the sound of the dawn call to prayer seeped into my ears, waking me to the dawn of Cairo's freezing winter. As a young boy of nine or ten, it was my daily ritual to jump out of my warm bed in my room on the top floor of the old and noble house that was our family home. I would follow the voice of my grandfather, Ali Abdel Razek, in his steady recitation of the Qur'an, until I arrived at his rooms located on the ground floor. He would acknowledge my greeting with a smiling nod, continuing his recitation of the holy book uninterrupted.

Once he had finished his recitation, we would fall into our playful banter of teasing and tickling each other like school children, with my grandfather seeming to magically cross an age gap of seventy years. I would then be seated in a corner and would watch him silently while he paced back and forth between his dressing room and the bath, grooming himself for the Fajr prayer, whilst reciting from memory his constant *zikr*.

Half a century later, this image of my grandfather, Sheikh Ali Abdel Razek or Ali Pasha Abdel Razek remains indelible in my memory. To this day, I have not encountered anyone who prays and prepares for prayer with the singular dedication of my grandfather. It seemed to me that he used to have a sacred daily date with his beloved Allah. I recall Ali Abdel Razek as a man who was gifted with everything: the gift of a true and solid belief; an enlightened mind; wisdom; a warm and generous heart; self-esteem; professional renown and recognition; and perhaps most of all, spiritual richness. However, despite these natural gifts, he was a most humble person. He lived his life preoccupied with his relationship to God.

Our traditional daily dinner was not like that of other Cairo families. In the household of Abdel Razek, the table comprised brimming platefuls of stewed vegetables and salads, what my uncles would sarcastically call "the daily plate of grass". Occasionally, these might be accompanied by cups of fresh yogurt, or cubes of locally made white cheese called Qareesh. The meal would be eaten with local dried bread that was brought in daily from Ali Abdel Razek's native village, Abu Jirj, in middle Egypt.

Islam and the Foundations of Political Power

This is how I remember my grandfather, Ali Abdel Razek, as a kind and loving, deeply devout and religious man.

When I reflect on his now famous book, *Al-Islām wa Uṣūl al-Ḥukm* or *Islam and the Foundations of Political Power*, I am always amazed that even today, close to a century after its publication, this invaluable essay still incites huge debates and impassioned responses. For me, every word and every phrase of the book are like weapons that confront and unveil the uncompromising religious misconceptions embraced by extremist political groups hiding behind the mantle of religion. These misconceptions have led to great turmoil and irreconcilable political factions almost all over the Arab and the Muslim worlds.

This book, especially in the final paragraphs, extends to fellow Muslims an invitation:

> There is not a single principle of the faith that forbids Muslims to co-operate with other nations in the total enterprise of the social and political sciences. There is no principle that prevents them from dismantling this obsolete system, a system which has demeaned and subjugated them, crushing them in its iron grip. Nothing stops them from building their state and their system of government on the basis of past constructions of human reason, of systems whose sturdiness has stood the test of time, which the experience of nations has shown to be effective.

A great many misleading conclusions about the essay still remain, one of which contends that it was addressed specifically to King Fouad, due to the coincidental publication of the book during a time when the king was attempting to reclaim the Egyptian throne and the seat of the caliphate. However, in the introduction, Abdel Razek states that his research for this book began in 1915, before Fouad became king and claimed the throne in 1917. Indeed, the fact that this essay still remains a subject of great discussion and debate seems to give it an almost universal relevance, taking it out of the specific and strictly local context of King Fouad's Egypt.

The word "secular" has come to the Arab lexicon since the turn of the twentieth century, bringing with it a host of meanings and interpretations. It was first introduced into Arab debates as the term *dariya*, which connoted a separation between religion and the state. This later evolved to become *la dini*, and now meant irreligious. In present-day circles secularism is often understood

A Tribute to Ali Abdel Razek

as *'ilmaniya*, and has become associated with immorality or the lack of ethics. Many contemporary scholars who perhaps have confused various notions and meanings of the idea of secularism have claimed that Abdel Razek was an advocate of secularism in this most negative sense, meaning that he was amoral. This is certainly not the case. My grandfather argued for the separation of religion from the state, as he clearly states in his essay. He could never have advocated irreligiosity or the slackening of moral values. He was a man of the highest integrity and he raised us, his family, with great moral uprightness and a deep and true awareness of the importance of the sacred and of belief in God. Should one wish to name or classify his practice of Islam, then we could say that his *"tariqah"* or way was that of following the sunna of the Prophet Muhammad in a simple and moderate manner. Perhaps we could even call him a Sufi, although he himself would never have been so bold as to name himself one.

Abdel Razek's book is an enlightened, scientific reading of the Qur'an – nothing less, nothing more. He used the holy book as his main point of reference. As a matter of fact, most of the chapters contain an on-going chain of verses drawn from the Qur'an, but related to the main concern of the book, which is governance in Islam. Equally, he makes consistent reference to a number of solid (*sahih*) hadiths. In fact, Ali Abdel Razek, the man and the thinker, steers far away from secularism – understood as a form of amoralism – and rather, stays very close to the teachings of the sunna of Muhammad. And this is how he raised us, his family. We learned a moderate Islam under his guidance, one that was based on ease, mercy and asceticism, or *zuhd*.

Another common, uncanny accusation alleges that Ali Abdel Razek did not write *Islam and the Foundations of Political Power* himself. Rather, it was written by someone else, and then given to Abdel Razek to publish in his name. What the advocates of this theory have overlooked is the fact that I possess the original handwritten manuscript of the book, with a lot of corrections, marginal notes and footnotes made by Ali Abdel Razek himself. These manuscripts are available as a sound reference for all those interested.

In this post-globalization era, and in the midst of all this turbulence and revolution, should we advocate political reform in the modern Muslim world, we ought to start by reading and understanding *Islam and the Foundations of Political Power*. This book can form the backbone of a sound, logical and scholarly inquiry into the question of political power as it pertains to Muslim societies.

Islam and the Foundations of Political Power

My belief is that every person is created with a mission in life. And no one passes away before fulfilling this mission, and thus satisfying his or her divine fate. *Islam and the Foundations of Political Power* was Ali Abdel Razek's heavy mission in the name of Islam and of humanity. He has fulfilled it perfectly. Moreover, he went on to live a long life afterwards, confident of having completed his mission and without ever altering a single word of the book.

God bless the soul of my beloved grandfather, and God bless the readers and scholars of his work.

Sincerely
Amr K. Hamed

Preface

Many scholars consider the publication of the essay *Islam and the Foundations of Political Power: an Inquiry into the Caliphate and Government in Islam* by Ali Abdel Razek[1] in 1925 to mark an important event in the contemporary history of Muslims. Not merely an exceptional intellectual or literary event, the publication of the book signalled an actual historical turning point, one that had a formative, long-lasting impact on the development of Muslim societies during the twentieth century.[2]

It was in the early 1990s that I learned, to my great surprise, that what in his time had been a ground-breaking work by Ali Abdel Razek still awaited translation into any of the major languages of Europe. By then, Islam had come to occupy centre stage in world awareness. Beyond the media, academics were turning their attention to contemporary expressions of thought, as well as to political movements in what is called the "Muslim world". A number of works by Muslim thinkers, translated into European languages, had become the object of extensive study in specialised circles. It was surprising to find that most of these works were representative of conservative, fundamentalist trends in Islam. Enormous attention was devoted to, among other things, trends that would later come to be grouped under the heading of Islamic fundamentalism.

This interest had significance beyond academia. It encouraged the idea that these thinkers were, in one way or another, "authentic" spokespersons for Muslims and Islam in the modern world. It also gave the impression that these works were representative of dominant, if not exclusive movements, of thought in Muslim contexts. This notion in turn influenced Muslim minds. The resulting distortion and misrepresentation is evident to anyone who is aware of the acute intellectual controversies which have been widespread in modern Muslim

---

1 No full translation of the essay into English has yet been published. Excerpts can be found in Charles Kurzman (ed.), *Liberal Islam: A Sourcebook*, New York: Oxford University Press, 1998. My own translation into French has been published as Ali Abdel Razek, *L'Islam et les fondements du pouvoir*, Paris: Éditions la Découverte, 1994.
2 For discussion of the impact of Abdel Razek's essay, refer to Mohammad 'Amara, *Al-Islam wa Uṣūl al-Ḥukm: dirassah wa watha'iq* ["Islam and the Foundations of Political Power: The Study and Documents"], Beirut: Al-Mu'assassa al-'Arabiya li al-Dirasat wa al-Nahr, 1972.

Islam and the Foundations of Political Power

contexts, and of the intensive debate instigated by publications that were neither conservative *nor* fundamentalist, but rather, critical and progressive. It was a deeply unsatisfactory state of affairs where essentialist and static-minded works by such reformers as Hassan al-Banna and Sayyid Qutb were available (some of them in multiple editions and various languages), and were widely read and commented upon, while others of equal, if not greater, importance and consequence in the modern Muslim world were wholly ignored. That *Islam and the Foundations of Political Power* by Ali Abdel Razek in particular, was not available in English (apart from short excerpts published in various anthologies) is indicative of this curious situation that has affected on-going debates about Muslims and the practice of Islam.

The present translation was conceived shortly after the publication of my French translation of Abdel Razek's essay in 1994. It has taken far too long, with many interruptions arising from administrative responsibilities (I could echo here what Ali Abdel Razek says about the circumstances of writing his book). Ms Maryam Loutfi volunteered a first set of translations from the Arabic into English. Shortly afterwards, I was lucky to come into close contact with Dr Aziz Esmail, former Dean and present Governor of the Institute of Ismaili Studies, who kindly agreed to undertake a complete rewriting with a view to rendering it into a plain and readable English. Using my French translation as a template, and referring where necessary to the Arabic original, he carried out the laborious task of what amounted to a fresh translation into English.

The result, to my mind, is a faithful rendering of a text which was after all not a scholarly disquisition in the technical sense (although it was based on meticulous attention to sources). Ali Abdel Razek's work is an *essay* in the best sense of the word. It interrogates and provides a perspective on prevailing interpretations of the Islamic past and attitudes about the relationship between politics and religion that have become widespread in contemporary contexts. It is a "historic" piece. In my introduction, I argue that it has played a significant role in shaping emerging debates about Islam and politics in Muslim contexts.

I would like to thank Sikeena Karmali Ahmed, Raahat Currim, Chloe Greenwood, Ashleigh Young, Charlotte Whiting, Mohamad Meqdad and Vera Pestell for their dedicated effort in preparing the manuscript for publication.

Finally, it must be emphasised that I alone bear the responsibility for any omissions or errors that may have gone undetected in the text.

Abdou Filali-Ansary

Introduction

Historical Background

The question of the caliphate, as it re-emerged in the 1920s, galvanised wide circles of people, mainly among learned elite Muslims. As an institution, the caliphate had until then experienced a rather turbulent thirteen-century history. It was created immediately after the death of the Prophet Muhammad to manage the community he had founded and to maintain the momentum created by the then new religious message. The title of caliph, meaning "deputy" or "successor", was also created shortly after the demise of the Prophet. It was initially given to some of the Prophet's prominent companions who had been co-opted by circles of influential members to lead the community. Each of the first four caliphs, considered afterwards by the Sunni majority as the "legitimate ones", was appointed in a different manner.[1]

Eventually, the caliphate was taken over by a succession of ruling families, beginning with the Umayyads and ending with the Ottomans. The change from co-opted and religiously inspired rulers, as they were later perceived, to a monarchical caliphate was considered by many in the community, and recorded later by historians, as a kind of *coup d'état*, constituting a violation of the principles associated with Islam and of the integrity and freedom of the *umma* or Muslim community. These monarchical systems which ruled over Muslim communities were generally accepted as more or less unavoidable. However, they were not considered to be fully legitimate. Over the centuries, the title of caliph lost its prestige. The Ottoman rulers, following many others, initially claimed for themselves the title of sultan or king rather than caliph. During the eighteenth century, at a time when their authority was seriously challenged, the Ottomans felt the need to reclaim the title of caliph. Early in the twentieth century when

---

1 Historical surveys of Islam's "founding moments" are numerous. Among the scholarly works that attempt an overall survey and understanding of the deep processes of change one should mention, in the English language, Marshall G. S. Hodgson, *The Venture of Islam: Conscience and History in a World Civilization*, Chicago, IL: University of Chicago Press, 1975 and Ira Lapidus, *A History of Islamic Societies*, Cambridge: Cambridge University Press, 2002. See also J. P. Berkey, *The Formation of Islam: Religion and Society in the Near East, 600–1800*, Cambridge: Cambridge University Press, 2003.

I

Islam and the Foundations of Political Power

Mustapha Kamal Atatürk took power of what remained of the once great Ottoman Empire, he first stripped the caliph of his temporal powers (1922) and then abolished the institution itself (1923).

The abrogation of the caliphate caused intense anxiety within the Muslim world. Already thrown off balance as a result of the impact of European colonialism on the traditional social and political order, Muslims were gripped by a great fear of the future. They did not know where the umma was headed after being deprived of the institution that had symbolised its continuity for centuries. The end of the caliphate, which had become the symbol of an "Islamic" polity – though often a remote, weak and disappointing one – signified to most Muslims the end of the world in which they had lived for centuries. As no religious or political alternatives to the caliphate were in sight, an overwhelming sense of loss ensued.

In a way, the loss of the caliphate returned the umma to the debate that dated back to the beginning of its history. Questions that had been more or less forgotten over the past thirteen centuries regained their relevance: how should Muslims organise themselves as a community? What system of governance should they adopt? Was the caliphate the only appropriate way to build and maintain an "Islamic" order? Was the caliphate an institution required by the tenets of the faith? Could the initial, authentic and legitimate caliphate be re-established? From the early nineteenth century, discussions about the modernisation of socio-political institutions had been gaining momentum and modern scholars paid great attention to these debates. These focused on processes of reform, however, rather than questioning the overarching framework for public life in the Muslim community. Ali Abdel Razek's essay, *Islam and the Foundations of Political Power*, brought the discussion back to the main question: how should Muslims organise themselves as a community?

At the time, deep changes were underway. Egypt, which had become an autonomous entity within the Muslim world centuries before, was entering a new era in its history. The confrontation between a foreign colonial power, Great Britain, and a strong nationalist movement were signalling the birth of the first modern, liberal polity in the Middle East. Following a scenario already familiar in the region, the king was pressing to re-establish traditional forms of political power, a system in which the monarch holds essential authority, while religious scholars known as the 'ulamā mediate between him and the population. The 'ulamā would enforce religious laws in civil matters and legitimise, to

Introduction

some degree, the political system. From the king's point of view, the rise of mass political movements, modern nationalist ideologies and their possible consequences, such as sovereignty of the people and the implementation of the rule of law were unacceptable. As a result, the king sought to rally traditional religious leaders and representatives of the high bourgeoisie in an effort to counter the mobilisation of the masses by the Wafd Party.[2]

Ali Abdel Razek's essay was a direct blow to the king's endeavours *and*, at the same time, a major challenge to the Wafd. From the perspective of Egyptian nationalists, Abdel Razek's ideas disturbed the political game by resuscitating basic questions that were thought to have been resolved or at least side-lined. In effect, he gave voice to an unexpected new argument in a political debate that had been largely restricted to the monarchy and the Wafd.

Consequently, modern political activists striving for independence, modernisation and democratisation – who should have been Abdel Razek's most enthusiastic supporters – were taken by surprise by his book. The Wafd was pursuing politics on a secular front, while benefiting from a rather favourable indifference from religious authorities. Egypt's nationalist project considered it potentially dangerous for the on-going political evolution of the country to reactivate political debates about religious terms and perspectives and their implications, however positive the new ideas might have been.

Two political games were being played at the same time. The first focused on the rejection of foreign subjugation and with it, the liquidation of traditional political forms that had made this subjugation possible in the first place. The second staked the adoption of modern political forms against the idea of rebuilding traditional ones. Liberal thinkers like Ali Abdel Razek found themselves in a delicate position. They opposed the traditional views and practices defended by the monarchy and the theologians, while *also* diverging from the popular movement that mobilised the masses in favour of populist ideologies which mainly proclaimed slogans about independence and emancipation.

What was important about this dilemma was that it brought to the fore points of view that profoundly differed from what had been known and recognised for centuries in traditional Muslim societies. As André Raymond has argued,[3] even

---

2 A nationalist political party created after the First World War and dissolved in 1952. It played an important role in the political life of Egypt for decades, acting as the "delegates" (the meaning of the Arabic word "Wafd") of the people in its fight to recover sovereignty from foreign powers.

3 *Égyptiens et français au Caire 1798–1801* ["The Egyptians and French in Cairo"], Paris: Institut français d'archéologie orientale, 1998.

Islam and the Foundations of Political Power

during a period of close proximity like the French occupation of Cairo in the aftermath of the Napoleonic expedition to Egypt in 1898, there was no effective exchange of ideas between European invaders and local intellectuals. He adds that nothing, or nearly nothing, changed in the way that indigenous societies viewed the natural and historical order of the world. With the exception of a very small elite, such as the chronicler Abdelrahman al-Jabarti,[4] local thinkers had not been able to access the intellectual world of the savants who accompanied the occupying forces.

However, roughly a century later, Muslims were becoming aware of other ways of looking at the world that embraced a better knowledge of the physical world, science and philosophy. A print press in the Arabic language had been born. A new "space of public communication" was created for the expression of ideologies, ambitions and desires that had originated in modern Europe, but had been infused with new life in non-European contexts. Debates about Islam and modernity shaped a new awareness, which was articulated by leading thinkers such as Jamal ad-Din al-Afghani[5] and Muhammad 'Abduh.[6] Muslim societies were no longer bound by their traditional views of the world. Initial advances towards the evolution of these new ideas were made by Arab Christians, who were the first to be receptive to modern European trends and to convey them to wider circles within the Arab world.

In this light, and for the first time in the modern history of Muslims, Ali Abdel Razek articulated a perspective that allowed for the examination of Islamic religious traditions from external, historical and critical points of view. This was to have major consequences. The first was a return to rationality as a pivot around which discussions about politics and religion would take place in ways that differed from the rational approaches previously adopted in the history of Muslim thought. In the early Muslim community, the rational analysis of religious matters had been, in a sense, common practice. Religious attitudes and obedience to divine commandments were initially understood as "requirements" of rationality in societies formerly bound by narrow traditions.

Rational thinking in early theology reached its peak with the Mu'tazilites and a host of other literate elites, who attempted to sketch rational perspectives about religious systems that could work as blueprints for Muslim forms of understanding and social order. Over generations, however, once an impressive

---

4 1753–1825.
5 1838–97.
6 1849–1905.

Introduction

corpus of theology and law had been endowed with authority, the implementation of reason in religious matters became progressively unacceptable and intolerable. Ali Abdel Razek hence spearheaded the return to a call to reason in religio-political matters. Implicitly, he challenged reformist and apologetic groups for whom rational discourse had to remain within the boundaries of established truths as they had been formulated within the domain of "tradition" and, furthermore, had been restricted to defending the faith against critics.

The reintroduction of reason in debates about religion also took place in the following decades by way of new disciplines, such as the humanities and social sciences. These new scholarly approaches would include historical critiques of canonical texts, the critical study of political and religious institutions, as well as commonly held perceptions and myths. They would function without paying heed to the authority of elders and of authoritative interpretations. A secularisation of world views and a form of disenchantment took place through the elaboration of new forms of knowledge.

Through the discussion initiated by Ali Abdel Razek, the ultimate criteria for truth came to be rationally supported views, rather than the established, authority-backed interpretations of revealed truth. This became a basic stake in the battle that Muslims were on the verge of engaging in, pitting reason, secular and free thought against the authority of tradition. Although Muhammad 'Abduh endeavoured to demonstrate the rationality of beliefs and practices associated with Islam, his attempt was to a large degree apologetic and limited by the need to restore the confidence and pride of Muslims in their own religious heritage. It was Ali Abdel Razek who made the first advances in the direction of applying processes of critical reasoning to what were considered to be religious matters that had been settled by authoritative tradition. He attempted to solve, *through critical inquiry*, an old dilemma that had created the most intense drama in the remote past of the Muslim community and one that was resurrected with the restoration and abolition of the caliphate.

The Abdel Razek Essay and its Immediate Impact

Ali Abdel Razek's ground-breaking essay, *Al-Islām wa Uṣūl al-Ḥukm*, is widely credited with having had a great impact on subsequent socio-political events across the Muslim world, generating what has been considered by some to be the greatest controversy in the modern history of Muslim societies. It created a kind of intellectual exchange that did not exist in traditional societies, involving

Islam and the Foundations of Political Power

polemics on a large, public scale and reaching out to popular opinion through the written press. One could argue that the intense conflict of interpretations generated by the book revived something similar to what Muslims had experienced in their early history: the *Fitna al-Kubra*, or Great Dissent, which had "broken" the community into the denominations – Sunni, Shi'a and Khawarij – that thrive to this day. The trauma of that age-old confrontation, which brought into existence deep and long lasting lines of division among Muslims, was still vivid in the collective memory.

The book led to the first trial of an intellectual for his ideas in modern times. The battle over the book raged in the press and was brought to court by the decision of King Fouad of Egypt, who was offended by it. Indeed, some parts of the book were very critical of despotism and the monarchical system in general. Moreover, it was understood that Abdel Razek ridiculed the ambition of reviving the title of caliph, an ambition that was nourished in many Middle Eastern royal courts of that time, including that of Egypt.

The court before which Ali Abdel Razek was tried was originally a disciplinary commission of the al-Azhar University for the oversight of the behaviour of its faculty members. The case of Ali Abdel Razek was the first to be brought before this institutional body, which had for the occasion called upon eminent traditional scholars and members of the faculty from al-Azhar. They were asked to determine whether the ideas presented in the book were acceptable from an orthodox point of view and whether the author could still hold onto his title of *'alim* (theologian). The fact that Ali Abdel Razek was a traditional scholar, whose role was understood as a guardian of orthodoxy, was clearly a source of discomfort for the authorities of the time. Not only were deeply held beliefs and prescriptions being challenged, they were being challenged by a then duly certified faculty member of al-Azhar University. He was later stripped of his title of *'alim* and had to observe a strict reserve; in fact, he seems to have suspended all research on the topic.

Islam and the Foundations of Political Power also resulted in a deep political crisis in Egypt. At the time, the Egyptian government was a coalition of two parties. The Liberal-Constitutionalists represented mainly landowners and the upper classes, which included many relatives and friends of Ali Abdel Razek. The second party in government had been created by the king to resist the overwhelming influence of the Wafd nationalist and populist political movement that enjoyed strong support among the population. The book provoked a deep

Introduction

disagreement between the two coalition partners. The Liberal-Constitutionalist Party, siding with Ali Abdel Razek, declared itself in favour of freedom of thought. The second party sided with the king and the traditionalists, rejecting Abdel Razek's views and urging his exclusion from all official functions. The Ali Abdel Razek case led to the eventual fall of the cabinet and the failure of the conservative, monarchist coalition. It became clear that the alliance of conservative and liberal ideologies was unable to offer a solid alternative to the nationalist and populist movements represented by the Wafd Party.

Furthermore, the book had a negative influence on attempts at the time to revive the institution of the caliphate. After the abrogation of the caliphate in Turkey by Mustapha Kamal Atatürk in 1923, prominent Muslim scholars and political activists began to call for reviving the caliphate, which was understood to be an essential institution for Muslims and a symbol of the unity and continuity of their community. It was chiefly in the "peripheries" of the Muslim world, in countries where Muslims were a minority, such as India or East Africa, that the need for restoring the caliphate was most intensely felt. However, it was mainly in the "central" areas, such as the Middle East, that the moral and political benefits of holding the title were perceived. The then kings of the Hijaz and Egypt competed for the title, and no agreement could be reached about who would next hold the title of caliph. Ali Abdel Razek, on the other hand, speaking as an al-Azhar scholar, argued that the caliphate was not a religious obligation for Muslims and that having been taken over by despots, it had in fact inflicted intense suffering and produced deep and devastating dissent within the community. This verdict on the part of Abdel Razek is believed by many to have impeded the revival of the caliphate and discredited the arguments of its supporters.

Perhaps one of the most important arguments regarding its influence on modern historical developments is that Abdel Razek's essay induced the birth of Islamist movements within Muslim societies as a reaction to on-going events and the way they were interpreted in his essay. Observers have pointed out a "troubling coincidence", linking the book's publication in 1925 to the creation in Egypt three years later of the Muslim Brotherhood, the first Islamist organisation in the modern Muslim world.[7] Was there a "cause and effect" relationship between these two events? Fundamentalism is seen as an outraged reaction of

---

7 See Mohammad 'Amara, *Al-Islam wa Uṣūl al-Ḥukm: dirassah wa watha'iq* ["Islam and the Foundations of Political Power: The Study and Documents"], Beirut: Al-Mu'assassa al-'Arabiya li al-Dirasat wa al-Nahr, 1972.

Islam and the Foundations of Political Power

pious Muslims to "Western-inspired" secularists who promote an alien system of thought, one which would strip Muslims of their identity, their faith and the very foundation of their worldview and social order.[8] The assumption of a historical link between the publication of Abdel Razek's book and the birth of Islamic fundamentalism is made by some who consider fundamentalism as a reaction and a *defence* against alien attempts at penetration and subversion of indigenous institutions and traditional expressions of thought, faith and so on.

Intimately linked to the previous points is the idea that Ali Abdel Razek was a precursor of secularist movements within Muslim societies. In fact, before 1925, during the nineteenth and early twentieth centuries, many endeavours to reform or modernise traditional institutions within Muslim societies were launched. They proposed, in one way or another, to reshape social and political institutions that had been under the control of religious clerics, in effect introducing some degree of secularisation. While a number of Muslim intellectuals supported this idea, the first clear defence of secularism through a fresh reading of the heritage came with Ali Abdel Razek's essay. Its thesis was subsequently adopted and supported by a line of thinkers, who although formulating different answers to the question of the relationship between religion and politics, considered Abdel Razek to be the initiator of a new and promising methodology of historical thinking in reinvestigating matters which had been assumed to be settled by Sunni dogma. It remained to be seen how such radical rethinking would evolve and what its influence on Muslim societies would be.

A New Theology?

As noted earlier, one of the most interesting facts in this debate was the office of Ali Abdel Razek as a traditional scholar, a member of the corps of 'ulamā, trained to preserve and implement religious conceptions and rules. He was the son of a notable, a wealthy landowner and a militant for the political modernisation of Egypt. Like his elder brother Mustafa, Ali received a complete course in traditional "Islamic" education. His opponents highlighted the fact that he had been "contaminated" by "Western" ideas when he undertook "secular" studies in the newly founded Egyptian University, shortly after receiving his *'alimiya* degree from al-Azhar University. He went on to Oxford University in Britain for

---

8 For details of this view of fundamentalism, see Hamid Enayat, *Modern Islamic Political Thought*, New York: ACLS Humanities, 2008 and Leonard Binder, "Ali Abdel Razek and Islamic liberalism", *Asian and African Studies*, 6(1), March 1982.

Introduction

further education, but had to interrupt his studies due to the outbreak of the First World War. Hence, his critics claimed that he had been exposed to "Orientalist" approaches, thus explaining his "deviation" from the orthodox path.

The striking fact about Abdel Razek's work is that, although it makes some explicit references to Western thinkers and Orientalists such as Hobbes and Locke, it does not show any direct influence of European thinkers. It is clear that he has an intimate knowledge of the key works that form part of the traditional Islamic corpus. He also had wide access to the latest writings by his contemporary scholars. At the same time, he does not seem to have a substantial knowledge of European political philosophy, nor of the works by the Orientalists on Islam. The only exception to this is the notable interest he shows in thinkers who had been "forgotten" or side-lined by mainstream scholarly trends in the Muslim world, and who had recently been "rediscovered" by European scholars, such as the Mu'tazila and Ibn Khaldun. Moreover, Abdel Razek's rationalist attitude is closer to that of the Mu'tazila and Ibn Khaldun than to any of the modern European scholars who had been fully exposed to the humanities and social sciences. In a way, his essay is a long reflection on the theories of Ibn Khaldun, who approached political power as an observable and complex reality rather than as a matter for broad and easy moralising. Therefore, the limited contact he had with Western thought may have "awakened" him from his "dogmatic slumber" and shown him that there were alternatives to the responses given by tradition. However, he remains a traditional scholar applying rational enquiry to matters thought to have been settled a long time ago.

Abdel Razek began to work on his essay during his immediate postgraduate years, but, as he indicates in his preface, he did not decide to publish it until events forced him to do so. What were these events? The abolition of the caliphate and the reaction it stirred up within traditional circles? The subsequent attempts to revive the caliphate? The apology for an "implicit Islamic constitution" by Rashid Rida?[9] The manoeuvres by King Fouad to divert the process of political modernisation? Probably all of these; the most significant of which was an innate disquiet caused by the collapse of fundamental institutions and the questioning of deeply entrenched views that had hitherto defined the framework of the public and private lives of Muslims. One may be tempted to believe that efforts to restore the caliphate and attempts to revive old symbols of

---

9 Rashid Rida, *Al-Khilāfa wal-Imāma al-'Uẓma* ["The Caliphate and the Great Imamate"], first published in 1924. See Simon Wood, *Christian Criticisms, Islamic Proofs: Rashid Rida's Modernist Defence of Islam*, Oxford: Oneworld, 2007.

Islam and the Foundations of Political Power

authority were perhaps the strongest incitement to the publication of this essay. However, certain parts of the essay seem to have been written taking into account the prevailing conditions in Egypt, especially those regarding the "nature" of the monarchical system. All the same, it remains the case that the ideas developed by Ali Abdel Razek, although situated in a specific historical context, are not entirely limited to this context. He questions the problem of *foundations of political power* at a time when the debate was entirely focused on discussions about prevailing concerns. Therefore, leaving aside what were perceived as unquestionable truths, he wanted to go *beyond* short-term concerns and reactions to consider certain essential questions from their very roots. Without intending to propose new theological interpretations, he nonetheless explores new ways of assessing fundamental issues of Islamic theology and of questioning some of the basic tenets of orthodox Sunni theology.

Abdel Razek's approach is striking in that it attempts to make a *tabula rasa* of everything considered to be unquestionable truth, particularly the narratives that surround "authentic" traditions associated with Islam. Traditional theologians usually develop their ideas within frameworks that they consider to be well-established truths. They attempt, smoothly and cautiously, to strengthen or attenuate certain notions within the framework of accepted principles. Their thought is often presented as a "commentary" or critique on some authority, whether a tradition, a conception or an author. Ali Abdel Razek does none of this. He proceeds with the approach of a rational scholar who, from a distinct and external perspective, examines established beliefs as given, observable phenomena in order to reach conclusions about the significance these beliefs may have for contemporary conditions.

He comes to the conclusion that Sunni Muslims maintained two different conceptions of the caliphate. Some, encouraged by "official" discourses, advocated it as a divinely originated power, sacred and unquestionable. Others saw the caliphate as a "contractual" system, where the caliph is a representative chosen by the community who exercises his power by virtue of a general consensus. This difference of opinion was usually held implicitly, in ambiguous terms, where the virtues of both models were advocated. However, Abdel Razek exposed in explicit terms widely accepted beliefs that had not been clearly conceptualised. This was the case with the theocratic implications of the first model, which saw the caliphate as a divinely ordained system, often "attenuated" with occasional references to the other, "contractual" one.

Introduction

Abdel Razek's objective is clear: to attain maximum clarity and expose the incoherence and inconsistency of some generally accepted views; while at the same time to reach conclusions that can be asserted with a fair degree of certainty. Critical reason became the basic instrument, reference point and authority by which "tradition" would be judged. This was precisely the opposite of what theologians had encouraged. In the later history of Muslim jurisprudence and theology, traditional schools used reason within the boundaries of what they considered to be established truths. They used reason as an instrument to settle technical problems arising in legal matters. However, they did not attempt to go any further than this.

When Ali Abdel Razek was a young man, Muhammad 'Abduh, one of the most influential reformists of the late nineteenth and early twentieth centuries, was propounding the idea that religion, and Islam more than others, was not opposed to reason. For 'Abduh, Islam was in fact the most "rational" of the great religions. He diagnosed that Islam in the nineteenth century, as it was practised by multitudes, was clouded by superstition and conformism. However, he believed that this could be eliminated by a return to the original attitudes of clear and simple principles by which the early generations of Muslims lived. He used reason apologetically, advocating on behalf of a proclaimed "truth" that would heal the consciousness of Muslims under the weight and humiliation of European domination. Reason was not used to search for truth, but rather to justify the truthfulness of inherited conceptions and to comfort anxious Muslim communities facing the onslaught of European powers and the need for rapid and deep change.

Distinctly, this was not the approach of Ali Abdel Razek who invoked reason as a tool and as the ultimate arbitrator in every discussion. Religious dogma was still accepted, but the associated narratives through which it was received and internalised were not. Although the dogma was accepted seemingly without question, the traditions that had been built around it and through which it had been formulated were submitted to open and direct scrutiny.

Theologians or traditional scholars were often asked to find justifications for already accepted, preconceived beliefs. Abdel Razek was critical of this view of the scholars' role. He came to a very bold conclusion: Muslims believe that the organisation of their community into a political entity is prescribed by their religion; however, the texts, traditions and even the example of the Prophet do not formulate any such obligation, nor do they provide anything that could be considered to be a constitution or a political prescription for the community. Rather, it was the

Islam and the Foundations of Political Power

theologians who strove to mobilise various and sometimes contrived strategies to "extract" or derive political indications from the sacred sources.

Ali Abdel Razek departs from the approach that prevailed in classical theology by arguing that it is more logical and respectful of the sources to admit that the political structures of Muslim communities belong to the history of Muslims rather than to the teachings of Islam as a religion. Therefore, Muslims should free themselves from what had been a harmful "myth" and a destructive institution – the caliphate and the monarchy lumped together – and from the idea that Islam imposes such forms on the Muslim community as the prescribed means of organising themselves as a community that conforms itself to the norms of Islam.

It is striking that as extreme rigour is sought through bold and innovative notions, Abdel Razek remains within the fold of traditional normative perspectives that have prevailed and continue to prevail in some circles within the Sunni community.

What were the Enduring Consequences?

The salient feature of Ali Abdel Razek's essay was to combine the attitude of the believer, based on the most reliable theological knowledge of the time, with the boldest questioning of what believers had associated with the creed regarding questions concerning the socio-political order. What he proposed fuses a strict adherence to the sacred texts and their explicit and visible message with the elimination – or at least rigorous rethinking – of some important conclusions that generations have drawn from them. This was, and still remains today, a direct blow to the conservative establishment.

Immediate reactions to the publication of Ali Abdel Razek's essay took the form of "refutations".[10] Three essays aimed at offering refutations to his reasoning and conclusions were published the same year (1925), and others were published subsequently. As mentioned before, there were also a number of other reactions: polemics in the print media; a trial before a disciplinary court; the fall of the coalition government; and the failure of the Muslim congresses to agree on a consensual response. The aftershocks can still be felt almost a century after the publication of *Islam and the Foundations of Political Power*. Reactions to Abdel

---

10 See Muhammad Al-Khidr Hussein, *Naqd Kitāb al-Islām wa Uṣūl al-Ḥukm* ["A Critique of the Book Islam and the Foundations of Political Power"], Cairo, 1925; or Muhammad Bakhit al-Matʻi, *Ḥaqīqat al-Islām wa Uṣūl al-Ḥukm* ["The Truth about Islam and the Foundations of Political Power"], Cairo, 1926.

Introduction

Razek's work continue to be published,[11] even though contemporary thinkers such as Khalid Muhammad Khalid[12] and Muhammad Ahmad Khalafallah[13] not only shared his basic views, but also developed sophisticated arguments in his defence. The rise of the fundamentalist tide has made a kind of pariah of Ali Abdel Razek, the emblem of what Muslims should never accept. Nevertheless, the challenge raised by his arguments remains.

Ali Abdel Razek reacted with great courage and firmness during the first months of the controversy surrounding his essay. A similar crisis was to be stirred up one year later when a book by Taha Hussein[14] about pre-Islamic poetry[15] raised questions about pre-Islamic history that pertained to the accepted narratives about the birth of Islam and its founding moments. Eventually, Ali Abdel Razek was obliged to retreat into total silence. He never withdrew or denounced his thesis as an error, as some other intellectuals did when faced with similar pressure. However, he was silenced and did not continue his research or publish any further on the subject. His title of 'alim, which had been revoked, was later restored under the liberal government formed in 1948. Nevertheless, he would not return to his profession or defend his authority as a religious scholar.

The case of Abdel Razek illustrates how repression and censorship operate in a context where no single institution has the exclusive responsibility for defending orthodoxy. The absence of such an institution does not mean that there is greater freedom of thought. Rather, the absence of a sole source of orthodoxy seems, on the contrary, to make the system tighter. When orthodoxy is not linked to a specific entity or corps, large numbers of individuals within the whole community *ipso facto* assume its defence. It becomes even more difficult to step outside the often implicit, mild but firm consensus that holds the community together. This pattern becomes apparent in subsequent cases of

---

11 It would be difficult to offer an exhaustive survey of such reactions. Suffice it to say that no work by an Islamist today would be devoid of critical mentions of 'Ali Abdel Razek.
12 1920–96. See his works *From Here We Start*, trans. Ismail R. el-Faruqi, Washington, DC: American Council of Learned Societies, 1953 (1st edn 1950) and *Al-Dawla fi al-Islam* ["Islam and the State"], Cairo: Dar Thabit lil-Nashr wa-al-Tawzi, 1989.
13 d. 1991. See his work *Al-Fann al-Qassassi fi al-Qur'an al-Karim* ["Narrative Art in the Venerable Qur'an"], first published in 1951. In 1947 Khalafallah presented a controversial doctoral dissertation to Cairo University about narrative art in the Qur'an. As a result of the critical attack that followed, he resigned from his teaching post at the university. A revised dissertation also proved unacceptable; the third revision, published as *Al-Fann al-Qassassi fi al-Qur'an al-Karim*, was reprinted several times. In this work he argues that the histories related in the Qur'an should be viewed as literary stories and that the welfare of the Muslim community should take precedence over Qur'anic texts.
14 1889–1973.
15 *Fil-Shi'r al-Jahili* ["On Pre-Islamic Poetry", 1926]. See also the edition published by Dar al-Nahr, 1996.

Islam and the Foundations of Political Power

religious controversy, one of the most recent being the case of Nasr Hamid Abu Zayd.[16] Sometimes individuals or a small group, who often represent an extreme activist segment of the community, voice concern over an author's alleged assault on the sacred beliefs and values of the community. This concern is echoed by a large and embarrassed silence from the majority, coupled with strident support from minority voices, thereby marginalising the critic who made the assault and eventually silencing him or her.

In the case of Ali Abdel Razek, there was not a popular manifestation against him in the immediate aftermath of the publication of his essay. This denotes a nuance of the attitude of "the masses". He faced traditionalist 'ulamā and some conservative voices in the political sphere rather than the pre-modern operatives through which controversies were conducted. Can we infer then that Ali Abdel Razek's attitudes towards despotism and his challenge to a certain politics at the core of the Islamic faith were more acceptable to the public? This is more than likely. Although with time Ali Abdel Razek seems to have become a pariah within conservative circles, during his own time he was a kind of moral winner, benefiting from the assent of the people while facing rejection from some elites.

Another long-term impact of Ali Abdel Razek's work has been more positively assessed. The adoption of a scholarly approach in dealing with issues considered until then as religious – and therefore amenable only to traditional theological handling – was to become an important trend in contemporary thought within predominantly Muslim contexts. It has transformed the heritage of Muslims – its theology, history, law and popular mythology – into an object of study for scholars both from within and outside the Muslim community. Eventually, the *secularised* humanities and social sciences made their way into the heritage of Muslim civilisations, deploying the full array of their conceptual tools and methodologies, although the analytical frameworks developed by most contemporary academics have not yet made their way to the public consciousness.

When they came to be applied to Muslim traditions, social and human sciences were already mature, secularised disciplines, in the sense that they were the outcome of a long evolution within Western, Christian and Jewish contexts. Religious dogmas, beliefs and perceptions were for them an object

---

16 1943–2010. In 1995, Abu Zayd was promoted to the rank of professor at Cairo University, but controversies about his academic work on the Qur'an led to a court decision of apostasy. It was claimed that Abu Zayd had renounced his Muslim faith through his writings, thus he was denied the promotion. As a supposed apostate (*murtadd*), he was also declared divorced from his wife, fellow academic Dr Ibtihal Younis. This decision forced the couple to leave their teaching posts at Cairo University.

Introduction

of study that was not conceded any kind of privileged status. The truth they sought was beyond any religious revelation or tradition, accessible only through rational investigation. Ali Abdel Razek was probably the first from within the Muslim community to submit its religious corpus to approaches of this kind and to attempt to solve one of its basic dilemmas through rigorous scholarly investigation.

Such an approach was the first of its kind in that it was an attempt at reforming prevailing views within Muslim contexts; this was to become an enduring trend from the early twentieth century onwards. The term "movement" does not apply here, since the sequence of scholarly endeavours that emerged did not display the features of a movement. However, it is striking to observe an unplanned, unconscious convergence among different parts of the community, all aimed at constructing alternative views of Muslim beliefs, and building new Muslim religious attitudes, by resorting to critical–historical approaches. Although communication within Muslim communities and across borders has benefited from modern technology, and new spaces of debate have emerged as a consequence, it should be noted that the division of the "Muslim world" into nation-states and the integration of these states into the new global order has created obstacles to a fluid communication on purely intellectual matters. And yet one finds great similarities in the disparate efforts of such thinkers as Mahmood Muhammad Taha,[17] Fazlur Rahman,[18] Abdelmajid Charfi[19] and Abdolkarim Soroush,[20] in which clear echoes of Ali Abdel Razek's ideas and approach can be perceived.

The Structure of the Essay

Regarding the formulation of his argumentation, Ali Abdel Razek visibly attempts to build a kind of logical or even *geometrical demonstration*. The essay is divided into "books", chapters and sections. Each section is numbered and given a title. At the outset of each chapter a list of points is provided, which is in fact a list of section titles. In this translation, we have maintained the way the

---

17 1909–85, author of *The Second Message of Islam*, Syracuse, NY: Syracuse University Press, 1996.
18 1919–88, author of *Islam and Modernity: Transformation of an Intellectual Tradition*, Chicago, IL: University of Chicago Press, 1982.
19 (1943–), author of *Islam: Between Message and History*, Edinburgh: Edinburgh University Press in association with Aga Khan University, 2009.
20 (1945–), author of *Reason, Freedom and Democracy in Islam: Essential Writings of Abdolkarim Soroush*, New York: Oxford University Press, 2000.

Islam and the Foundations of Political Power

text was presented in its original Arabic version. The entire essay is engineered as a structured, rational enquiry progressing step by step to the final conclusion. In a way, Abdel Razek's writing style is strikingly reminiscent of the style adopted by rational philosophers such as Baruch Spinoza in his *Ethics* (1677) and logicians such as Ludwig Wittgenstein in his *Tractatus Logico Philosophicus* (first published in German in 1921 as *Logisch-Philosophische Abhandlung*, with English translations in 1922 and 1961). Ali Abdel Razek introduced footnotes in his text and this was quite an innovation in the writing style adopted by traditional scholars. However, the information provided in the footnotes is not detailed and does not comply with the conventions that are followed in scholarly publications today. Abdel Razek assumed that his audience, which included his peers – theologians, scholars, judges and lawmakers, as well as politicians – would have been familiar with the texts to which he refers, in the same way that an early twentieth-century essay written in Europe with references to Saint Thomas Aquinas or Nietzsche would be readily understood without necessarily requiring further reference details. Abdel Razek's sources include sometraditional classics, such as books of hadith, *The Muqaddimah* of Ibn Khaldun and a number of treatises widely used in academia during his time. We know that most of these sources were published in Arabic with no English translation available.

For the sake of clarity, this volume includes a list of Abdel Razek's sources with full publication details. The text also includes some explanatory notes, in square brackets, beside Abdel Razek's original footnotes. Additional notes are provided about particular people, events or vocabulary that may be unfamiliar to modern readers; these notes are indicated with asterisks. Readers may find, however, that Abdel Razek's argument is such that exact references may not be needed to comprehend his logic.

In form as well as in substance, the essay represented a major turn in breaking with traditional discourses. This may explain the shock that it produced. This becomes especially true when one bears in mind that Muslim scholarly circles from the tenth century onwards produced mainly commentaries on earlier works, glosses and summaries, some in verse form, built upon the assumption that the important matters had been settled by early masters and all that remained for later generations was to strive to understand and assimilate.

On the other hand, the perspective taken by Abdel Razek assumes that normative judgements made within Sunni theological schools are the standard

Introduction

and authentic representation of Muslim views. He often combines all other views – Shi'a, Kharijites and Mu'tazila – in one broad category under a label used by traditional Sunni theology, such as *rawafidh* (rejectionists), to refer to all those who rejected the assumptions of Sunnism. In his attempt to reach scholarly detached views, he did not go as far as to take seriously the diversity of interpretations that emerged in the history of Muslims. Historically it has been, and continues to be today, a reflex among many Muslim thinkers, often passed onto non-Muslim scholars, to assume that the Sunni interpretation sets the standard and that there is one broad unit called Islam that can be discussed from one main or even unique perspective, discarding variants that are considered "unorthodox". Ali Abdel Razek does refer to "variants" within the Muslim tradition, but he does so by using the terminology of Sunni authorities. As a result, he shares an attitude that does not rise to the standards of the scholarly and rigorous approach that he strives to attain. Paradoxically, while he takes an approach more in line with modern scholarly trends, including the "rediscovery" of the Mu'tazila and of Ibn Khaldun, he remains deeply rooted in attitudes proper to traditional Sunni circles, where the Shi'a and others are seen as remote and marginal "sects".

Islam and the Foundations of Political Power

Foreword

In the name of God, the Most Merciful, the Compassionate.
I bear witness that there is no god but God. I worship and fear none but Him. All but Him are as nothing. Unto Him is the power and the glory. Praise be to Him in this world and the next. He is my only recourse, and my best protector. I bear witness too that Muhammad is the Messenger, sent as a witness, a giver of glad tidings and warnings, to summon humankind to God, and be a guiding light to them. May God's peace be upon him, and may he be in peace.*

In the year 1333 AH [1915] I was appointed a judge in the Islamic courts of Egypt and subsequently began developing an interest in the history of Islamic jurisprudence.

Jurisprudence, with all its branches, is an instrument of governance. Its history is closely linked to that of the political establishment. Moreover, Islamic jurisprudence is a key element of Islamic government. Therefore, if we wish to understand the institution of Islamic jurisprudence, it is first necessary to understand the basis upon which it has been founded; in other words, to understand the nature of political authority in Islam.

It is generally believed in Islam that all power resides with the caliphate, the supreme imamate. Therefore, I have decided to begin this work with an investigation of the caliphate – something which I initiated many years ago. I now feel, however, that I have barely accomplished anything significant, as all I have managed to produce at the end of what was truly a laborious task are these few pages. It is with the utmost humility, therefore, that I present them to the interested reader.

These pages are meant to be an introduction to the study of the history of jurisprudence. They cover all the principal conclusions I have reached concerning the caliphate and the theory of political power in Islam. I do not claim to have exhausted this topic in all its aspects, or to have achieved anything beyond a

---

* This is a ritual prayer formula with which Muslim theologians would open their essays.

Islam and the Foundations of Political Power

general treatment of the subject. At times, I have had to satisfy myself with statements that may appear evasive or allusions that may seem vague.

I earnestly wish to be able to amend the weaknesses of this work, which I am the first to acknowledge. And if that is not possible, I will have at least provided new ideas on the subject; ideas which I express to other scholars with the utmost candour and honesty. I hope, too, that this work will offer a starting point for further elaboration and that it may propel those who remain unclear about these questions to look for further answers.

That being said, I must state that these pages are the fruit of a labour in which I have invested the better part of my energies for many years. These years have been difficult; full of forced interruptions, worries and loss of heart. I might, for example, work for a day, only to find that events outside my control obliged me to put off the job for several days. I might return to it for a month, only to find myself having to interrupt it once again, for several months at a stretch. Naturally, therefore, the work as it stands now falls well short of the quality I had intended it to have. All the same, it represents my best efforts and the best conclusions that I was able to reach.

> God charges not any soul except with what it can bear. To its credit belongs what it has earned: upon it falls the burden of what it has deserved.
> Our Lord,
> Take us not to task if we forget or err.
> Our Lord,
> Do not lay upon us a heavy burden, as You laid upon those who came before us.
> Our Lord,
> Do not lay upon us what we have no power to bear.
> Pardon us, forgive us, be merciful towards us.
> You are our Patron, so grant us Your support against the impious.[1]

Ali Abdel Razek
Mansoura, Friday, Ramadan 7, 1343 [1 April 1925]

---

1 Qur'an 2.286. [*The Qur'an: A New Translation*, trans. Tarif Khalidi, Penguin Classics: London, 2006. All Qur'anic verses are taken from this translation and are referenced as Qur'an *sura.aya*; chapter number.verse number.]

Book One

The Caliphate and Islam

1
The Nature of the Caliphate

Linguistic origins of the word "caliphate" – Conventional usage – The significance of the theory of the Prophet's deputyship – Explanation for the choice of the term – The rights of the caliph according to common belief – On whether the caliph's prerogatives are defined in religious law (shari'a) – Caliphate and monarchy – Origins of the caliph's power – The theory according to which the caliph derives his power directly from God – The theory that the caliph derives his authority from the people – Prevalence of the same difference of opinion among thinkers in the West

1. The root form of the word "caliphate" has the sense of deputising for someone, succeeding him or following in his wake. It also means performing an office in lieu of another, whether in the latter's presence or absence.

Had We willed We could have created you as angels, to take your place on earth.[1]

Khilafa (caliphate), then, is a "standing-in" for someone who happens to have died, is ill or incapacitated. The plural of *khilafa* is *khala'if*, while the plural of *khailifa* (caliph) is *khulafa*.[2] The caliph is the supreme holder of power (sultan).[3]

2. In Muslim usage, the term "caliphate", for which the term "imamate" is used as a synonym, refers to an overall leadership of the community in spiritual as well

---
1 Qur'an 43.60.
2 Definitions given by Al-Isfahani in his *Al-Mufradāt fī Gharīb al-Qur'ān* ["Rare Terms in the Qur'an", c. 1109].
3 See dictionaries, collections of hadith and other reference works.

Islam and the Foundations of Political Power

as temporal affairs by a successor to the Prophet.[4] Al-Baydawi[5] offers a similar definition: "The imamate is the office of someone who deputises for the Prophet, with a view to the observance of the religious law (sharī'a) and defending the community through means that it is obliged to follow."[6]

Ibn Khaldun explains this as follows: "And to exercise the caliphate means to cause the masses to act as required by religious insight into their interests in the other world as well as in this world. The worldly interests have bearing upon the interests in the other world, since according to the Lawgiver (Muhammad); all worldly conditions are to be considered in their relation to their value for the other world. Thus, the caliphate in reality substitutes for the Lawgiver (Muhammad), in as much as it serves, like him, to protect the religion and to exercise (political) leadership in the world."[7]

3. According to the sources mentioned above, the office of the caliph substitutes the office of the Prophet, who during his lifetime was entrusted with a religious mission arising from divine revelation. He was charged with maintaining the Message of Islam and implementing its tenets, transmitting it from God to the people and summoning them towards Him.

These scholars think that God appointed the Prophet Muhammad to propagate the truth, to convey the tenets of His holy law to humanity and simultaneously, to preserve the religion and conduct temporal affairs in accordance with its principles.[8]

Upon the death of the Prophet, the caliphs succeeded him in both of his roles: as a custodian of the religion, and in the regulation of the community's quotidian affairs in accordance with the principles of the faith.

4. The name *imam* is derived from the comparison (of the caliph) with the leader (imam) of prayer, since (the caliph) is followed and taken as a model, just

---

4 See Abd as-Salam al Laqani's commentary, *Ithāf al-Murīd bi-Sharah Jawharat at-Tawḥīd* ["The Disciple's Contribution to Commentary on the Essence of Divine Unity", 1831] on Abd as-Salam's *Sharh Jawharāt at-Tawḥīd* ["Explaining the Essence of Divine Unity", c. 1276].
5 His full name is Nassir al-Din Abu Said Abdallah ibn Umar ibn Muhammad al-Shirazi al-Baydawi. Died in 791 AH [1388].
6 Refer to the book by the latter titled *Ṭawāli' al-Anwār min Maṭāli' al-Anẓār* [Al-Baydawi, "Manifestations from the Perspectives of the Horizon", c. 1300]. [This is a summary of Zamakhshari's *Al-Kashāf al-Tanzil*, c. 1132.]
7 Ibn Khaldun, *The Muqaddimah*, vol. 1, pp. 387–8 [trans. Franz Rosenthal, Chichester: Princeton University Press, 1967. All subsequent quotations from the *Muqaddimah* refer to this edition].
8 Ibn Khaldun, *The Muqaddimah*, vol. 1, pp. 387–8.

The Nature of the Caliphate

like the prayer leader. Therefore (the caliphate) is called the "great imamate".

The name "caliph" (khalifah) is given to the caliph, because he represents (*kh-l-f*) the Prophet in Islam. One uses "caliph" alone, or "caliph of the Messenger of God". There is a difference of opinion concerning the use of "caliph of God". Some consider (this expression) permissible as derived from the general "caliphate" (representation of God) of all descendants of Adam, implied in the verse of the Qur'an, "I shall appoint a deputy on earth" (Qur'an 2.30) and the verse, "It is He Who made you inheritors of the earth" (Qur'an 6.165). But, in general, it is not permissible to use (the expression "caliph of God"), since the verse quoted has no reference to it (in connection with the caliphate in the specific sense of the term). Abu Bakr forbade the use (of the expression "caliph of God") when he was thus addressed. He said, "I am not caliph of God, but the caliph (representative, successor) of the Messenger of God."[9]

5. Nevertheless, these scholars suggest that the caliph assumes the same position as the Prophet towards the faithful. He is expected to govern their affairs and is entitled to receive their unconditional obedience while exercising absolute sovereignty over them. It is the duty of the caliph to ensure strict observance of religious principles, to implement the legal provisions contained in the shari'a and to administer the affairs of the community.

On their part, the faithful are expected to show love and devotion to the caliph as he is the successor to the prophet whose position, in the eyes of Muslims, is that of the noblest individual. The caliph therefore becomes entitled to the respect due to a representative of the Prophet; the supreme overseer and defender of the faith. As protecting the Message [of Islam] is a task of supreme importance, one who is entrusted with this religious duty carries a mission of the greatest nobility and dignity.

According to several hadiths, the faithful are obliged to listen to the caliph and to obey him both "outwardly and inwardly".[10] For obedience to the imam is equivalent to obedience to God; while disobeying him is tantamount to disobeying God.[11] The obligation of offering counsel to and obeying the imam is

---

9   Ibn Khaldun, *The Muqaddimah*, pp. 387–8.
10 See the commentary of Al-Bajuri on *Al-Jawhara*. [The commentary is entitled *Sharḥ Jawharāt at-Tawḥīd*, "Explaining the Essence of Divine Unity", c. 1276.]
11 A tradition attributed to Abu Hurayra. See Ibn 'Abd Rabbuh, *Al-'Iqd al-Farid*. ["The Unique Necklace", c. 860–940. Abu Hurayra (603–81) was one of the Prophet's companions to whom many hadith reports were attributed by later hadith collectors.]

Islam and the Foundations of Political Power

a religious duty and a necessity. Faith is not complete, nor the profession of the Islamic faith fulfilled, until this duty is realised.[12]

In sum, the person endowed with the authority of the caliph thus becomes the successor of the Messenger of God. He represents the power of God[13] as His shadow on earth. His authority over Muslims, like the authority of God Himself or His Prophet, becomes absolute. It is not surprising therefore, that he should proclaim power over the souls and the goods of men.[14]

It follows that the caliph is the only person entitled to command and to forbid; as well as to administer the major and minor affairs of the umma. Any other authority that is hierarchically inferior to the caliph, then, must derive from him. Any secondary function is encompassed within the caliph's own authority. All duties, whether religious or worldly, belong to his office. For, "It has become clear that to be caliph in reality means acting as substitute for the Lawgiver (Muhammad) with regard to the preservation of the religion and the political leadership of the world":[15] "The caliphate is a kind of mainspring and comprehensive basis, and all these (functions) are branches of it and fall under it because of the wide scope of the caliphate, its active interest in all conditions of the Muslim community, both religious and worldly, and its general power to execute the religious laws relative to both (religious and worldly affairs)".[16]

The caliph does not share his authority with anyone else. He alone has authority over Muslims, except for that which he delegates to others. Personages such as judges, governors, moral guardians and all other officers in charge of the affairs of Muslims are subordinates of the caliph. He alone is entitled to appoint or dismiss them, and is the only person with the right to define the scope and boundaries of their prerogatives.

6. It may seem, from the work of these scholars and their definition of the caliphate, that the caliph's authority is confined to ensuring a strict observance of the edicts of the sharī'a; which he is required to enforce and which he would

---

12 *Ibid.*
13 In a speech given at Mecca, the Caliph Al-Mansur said: "O people, I represent the power of God on earth, I lead you with His support, His guidance and His backing. I am also the guardian of His treasury, for which I act following His will and decision, distributing His allocations with His agreement, since He made me a trustee in charge of overseeing it" (*Al-'Iqd al-Farīd*).
14 See Al-Baydawi, *Ṭawāli' al-Anwār min Maṭāli' al-Anẓār* ["Manifestations from the Perspectives of the Horizon", c. 1300].
15 Ibn Khaldun, *The Muqaddimah*, p. 448.
16 Ibn Khaldun, *The Muqaddimah*, p. 449.

by no means infringe upon. He is duty-bound to guide Muslims along a single, unique path, distinct from all others. This is a straight, unwinding path, defined by the principles, objectives and guidelines that are unequivocally laid down in the sharī'a; thus making it impossible for the faithful to go astray. Furthermore, these same principles, objectives and guidelines also prevent the caliph from either deviating from the sharī'a or abusing his power. This is understood as the path of the Islamic faith shown to Muslims long ago by the Prophet Muhammad. It is the path outlined in the Book of God, the traditions of His Prophet and the consensus [*ijmā*] of Muslims.

The theologians discussed earlier, believe that the caliph's authority is rigorously restricted by the sharī'a. They consider this a sufficient safeguard against potential abuses or deviations on his part. Some go as far as to assert that if a caliph happens to commit an injustice, or to compromise himself through debauchery, he would *de facto* disqualify himself.

7. For this reason, Muslim scholars have made a distinction between caliphate and kingship. (To exercise) natural royal authority means to cause masses to act as required by purpose and desire. (To exercise) political (royal authority) means to cause the masses to act as required by intellectual (rational) insight into the means of furthering their worldly interests and avoiding anything that is harmful (in that respect). (And to exercise) the caliphate means to cause the masses to act as required by religious insight into their interests in the other world as well as in this world.[17]

Thus, Ibn Khaldun came to conclude that a genuine caliphate existed only during the first era of the Islamic State and up to the end of 'Ali's reign.

> It has thus been shown how the form of government came to be royal authority. However, there remained the traits that are characteristic of the caliphate, namely, preference for Islam and its ways, and adherence to the path of truth. A change became apparent only in the restraining influence that had been Islam and now came to be group feeling and the sword. That was the situation in the time of Mu'awiyah, Marwan, his son 'Abd-al-Malik, and the first Abbasid caliphs down to ar-Rashid and some of his sons. Then, the characteristic traits of the caliphate disappeared, and only its name remained. The form of government came to be royal authority pure and

---

17 Ibn Khaldun, *The Muqaddimah*, p. 387.

Islam and the Foundations of Political Power

simple. Superiority attained the limits of its nature and was employed for particular (worthless) purposes, such as the use of force and the arbitrary gratification of desires and for pleasures.

This was the case with the successors of the sons of 'Abd-al-Malik and the Abbasids after al-Mu'tasim and al-Mutawakkil. They remained caliphs in name, due to the continuation of "the spirit of collective solidarity" [assabiya] among the Arabs. In these two stages caliphate and royal authority existed side by side. Then, with the disappearance of the spirit of collective solidarity and the annihilation of the (Arab) race and complete destruction of (Arabism), the caliphate lost its identity. The form of government remained royal authority pure and simple.

This was the case, for instance, with the non-Arab rulers in the East. They showed obedience to the caliph in order to enjoy the blessings (involved in that), but royal authority belonged to them with all its titles and attributes. The caliph had no share in it. The same was done by the Zanatah rulers of the Maghrib. The Sinhajah, for instance, had just such a relationship with the 'Ubaydid (Fatimids), and the Maghrawah and also the Banu Yafran (Ifren) with the Umayyad caliphs in Spain and Ubaydid (Fatimids) in al-Qayrawan.

It is thus clear that the caliphate first existed without royal authority. Then, the characteristic traits of the caliphate became mixed up and confused. Finally, when royal authority came to exist alone its spirit of collective solidarity had separated from the spirit of collective solidarity of the caliphate."[18]

8. Having attributed so much power to the caliph's position, and having raised it to such exalted heights, the scholars ought to have informed us of the source of the power imputed to the caliph. Furthermore, they ought to have explained from where it sprang – who bequeathed this power to the caliph? However, the fact is that these scholars neglected to follow this manner of enquiry, just as they neglected the study of other political subjects that might have placed the caliph's position into question, or under discussion. Nevertheless, upon reading some of the relevant statements of these scholars, we may infer that Muslims have adopted two theories regarding the matter of the caliphate.

---

18 See the chapter, "Transformation of the caliphate into a monarchy" in Ibn Khaldun, *The Muqaddimah*, pp. 427–8.

9. The first theory, widely shared among Muslim scholars and by the general public, asserts that the caliph derives his authority and power directly from God. All the studies and treatises regarding the caliphate concur with this point of view and refer to this belief. As indicated above,[19] Muslim scholars have interpreted the caliph as the shadow of God on earth. Abu Ja'afar al-Mansur went so far as to presume that he was God's power on Earth.*

This opinion was widely spread among Muslims. Religious scholars and poets have proclaimed it from the early years of Islam. They attested that it was God Himself who appointed the caliph, and bequeathed His authority to him, as illustrated in the following verses:

> He became the caliph
> Or rather the caliphate
> was destined for him –
> Like Moses
> Who was destined
> To approach God.

Another poet, speaking in the same vein, said:

> God entrusted it to you
> For the betterment
> And the salvation
> Of the community.**

Again, in the same vein, Al-Farazdaq[20] said:

> Hisham,[21] God's chosen one
> For the people,

---

* See Peri J. Bearman *et al.* (eds), *Encyclopaedia of Islam*, 2nd edn, 12 vols, Leiden: E. J. Brill, 1960–2005.
** These excerpts of poetry were popular during the classical period.

19 *Ibid.*, paragraph 5.
20 Abu Firas, Humam ibn Ghalib ibn Sa'sa'a, reputed to have lived for over a hundred years, died in Basra in 110, 112 or 114 AH [728, 730 or 732]. [Al-Farazdaq's poetry collections include *Dīwān al-Farazdaq* ["The Anthology of Farazdaq"], c. 720 and *Naqā'iḍ bayna al-Jarir wal-Farazdaq* ["The Polemic Poem between al-Jarir and Farazadaq"], c. 720.]
21 Hicham ibn Abd al-Malik was the tenth Umayyad caliph. He died in Rusafa in 125 AH [743] at the age of fifty-five.

> For whom darkness withdraws
> From all over the earth,
> The sky to which they look,
> Praying for rain.

This point of view led the poets to such exaggeration as to exalt the caliphs to the rank, or near rank, of the Divine Being. Thus, one of the poets says:

> It is what you will, not what destiny wills.
> Command as you will, for you are the One, the Omnipotent.

Praising al-Walid ibn Yazid,* Tarih said:[22]

> You are the son of the vast plains.
> Never have you been confined in the depths of any vales.
> Praised be your ancestors from here and from there,
> Praised be your noble origins.
> If you order the floods to divert from their course,
> Topped by waves high as mountains,
> They will scatter, withdraw, turn aside from your path.

If, on the other hand, one examines the writings of several religious scholars ['ulamā], especially after the fifth century of the hijra, one finds that they begin their work by mentioning a king or potentate. Invariably, they place him above the rest of humankind, crediting him with quasi-divine qualities. This is illustrated in the preamble to *Ar-Risāla ash-Shamsīya fil-Qawā'id al-Manṭaqīya*,** by Najm al-Din al-Qazwini:[23]

> He thus beckoned to me: the one who enjoys the solicitude of the Supreme Being, who has the exclusive benefit of Divine support, towards whom everyone gravitates, and attachment to whom carries advantage to those who obey as well as disobey.

---

* Eleventh caliph of the Umayyad dynasty. He ruled from 743 to 744 and was killed in 744.
** c. 1276.
22 Tarih ibn Ismail Naqfi chanted for Al-Walid ibn Yazid (an Umayyad) and later for Abu Jaafar al-Mansur (an Abbasid). See *Kitāb al-Aghānī*. ["The Book of Songs", an encyclopaedic collection of poems and songs by the scholar Abu i-Farai al-Isfahani, 897–967.]
23 Known as the Katibi. Died in 493 AH [1100].

The Nature of the Caliphate

Likewise, Al-Qazwini's critic, Qutb al-Din al-Rāzī,[24] begins his commentary with the following:

> I have sought through this work to serve the one who has been graced by God's holy spirit, and who has been divinely appointed in command of men ... the one whose face bears signs of eternal felicity and the tokens of divine favour, the nobility of truth of the state and religion; the wise man of Islam, to Muslims, a guide.

Abd al-Hakim al-Sialakuti[25] says in his gloss concerning the above-mentioned commentary:

> I have made this work a gift to the one chosen by God for eternal sovereignty, favoured by his supreme support ... the propagator of the true faith, the founder of the principles of the Holy Law, the shadow of God in the two lands, the saviour of Islam and of Muslims, the builder of God's nations, the successor to the Prophet, graced with divine support and victory ...[26]

In sum, the theory according to which the caliph derives his authority from God was dominant in the discourse of the theologians; hence, it became widespread among Muslims.

10. According to another theory, upheld by some scholars and expounded at length, the caliph derives his authority from the umma, which designates and confers sovereignty on him. Al-Hutay'a[27] seems to favour this theory. Addressing Umar ibn al-Khattab, he said:

> You are the Imam to whom, after his companion,
> Men entrusted the reins of authority.
> In choosing you it was not you they favoured,
> It was for their own sake that they did so.

---

24 Qutb al-Dīn Mahmud ibn Muhammad ar-Rāzī. Died in 466 AH [1033]. *Ar-Risāla ash-Shamsīya fīl-Qawā'id al-Mantaqīya* ["The Dazzling Work on the Foundations of Logic", 1948].
25 Qadi 'Abd al-Hakim al-Sialakuti. Died in 1067 AH [1657] and was buried in Sialakut.
26 See the collection published by Sheikh Faraj Allah Zaki al-Kurdi in 1323 AH [1905]. [The author is alluding to a collection that is no longer available.]
27 Jarual ibn Aws ibn Malik, died around 30 AH [650].

Islam and the Foundations of Political Power

The most complete exposition of this theory along with its most categorical defence can be found in the treatise entitled *Caliphate and the Sovereignty of the Nation*, published by the Turkish Grand National Assembly in Ankara.[28]

11. A similar disagreement to that among Muslims regarding the basis of the ruler's power emerged among Europeans and had a considerable impact on their history. The first of the theories discussed above bears a resemblance to the ideas of Thomas Hobbes,[29] to the effect that "the power of kings is sacred and divinely ordained". The second theory is quite similar to the ideas of John Locke on this topic.[30]

We hope, in this first chapter, to have given a sufficient account of the significance attached by Muslim scholars to the caliphate, particularly of the belief according to which the caliphate denotes "the management of worldly and religious affairs by a delegate of the Prophet".[31]

---

28 Translated into Arabic by Abd-al-Ghani Sunni and published in Egypt in 1924. [*Caliphate and the Sovereignty of the Nation* was an attempt by a group of religious lawyers to provide a religious justification for the change in government in Turkey in 1922. On behalf of the Turkish Grand National Assembly, the lawyers issued a statement which reasoned that the change was in harmony with the Qur'an.]
29 Thomas Hobbes, 1588–1679. See Arthur Kenyon Rogers, *A Student's History of Philosophy*, 1901.
30 John Locke, 1632–1704. See Arthur Kenyon Rogers, *A Student's History of Philosophy*, 1901.
31 Saad Eddin Taftazani, *Maqāṣid at-Ṭālibīn fī Ilm Uṣūl ad-Dīn*. ["The Aims of Students and the Foundations of Faith", 1383.]

2
The Status of the Caliphate

The proponents of the necessity of the caliphate – The opponents of this theory – The arguments of the former – The Qur'an and the caliphate – Resolution of doubts surrounding some verses of the Qur'an – The tradition (sunna) and the caliphate – Refutation of the arguments of those who claim that justification can be found in the sunna

1. The scholars discussed in Chapter 1 considered the appointment of a caliph to be a binding duty; they believed that to do otherwise would be to commit a sin. Nevertheless, these scholars disagree on whether the basis of the caliphate is rational or legal. However, this is not the issue we are interested in here. Rather, we are concerned most notably with the fact that the necessity of the caliphate was so widely accepted that Ibn Khaldun himself claimed it was a question to be settled by consensus or ijmā.

2. Ibn Khaldun argues: "Some people have taken the exceptional position of stating that the position of imam is not necessary at all, neither according to the intellect nor according to religious law. People who have held that opinion include the Mu'tazilah al-Asamm and certain Kharijites, among others. They think that it is necessary only to observe the religious laws. Those (who so argue) are refuted by the general consensus.[1]

3. These scholars present various arguments as outlined below in support of the idea that the caliphate is essential:

---
1 Ibn Khaldun, *The Muqaddimah*, pp. 390–1.

Islam and the Foundations of Political Power

First, the consensus of the Prophet's companions:

> At the death of the Prophet, the men around him proceeded to render the oath of allegiance to Abu Bakr and to entrust him with the supervision of their affairs. And so it was at all subsequent periods. In no period were people left in a state of anarchy. This was so by general consensus, which proves that the position of imam is a necessary one.[2]

Secondly, the appointment of an imam is:

> a prerequisite for the due maintenance of worship and the well being of the governed. It is equivalent to the enjoining of the right and prohibition of the wrong, both of which are, without doubt, religious duties. Unless an imam is appointed, these duties cannot be performed, nor can the affairs of the governed be organised. Without them, voluntary gifts are replaced by confiscations, injustice proliferates, chaos prevails, and the antagonisms inherent in human society remain unresolved. No doubt, whatever is essential for the discharge of a duty itself becomes a duty. Consequently, the appointment of an imam becomes a duty. Its character as a duty may be deduced in the same manner as the obligation to observe, within the bounds set by the Lawgiver, the six fundamental rules – the protection, namely, of the faith, of human life, of reason, of the integrity of lineage, of property and of honour.[3]

4. None of the scholars who attested that the appointment of an imam was a religious duty could substantiate this thesis with a verse from the Qur'an. If such a verse had existed, the scholars concerned would not have hesitated to utilise and expound it at length. Had there existed a mere shred of evidence in favour of the thesis of the imamate as an obligation, the more zealous among the proponents of the caliphate would have taken this hint as complete proof. However, the scholars, whether neutral or partial to the caliphate, were unable to find any arguments in favour of their thesis in God's book. Therefore, they satisfied themselves with the legal thesis that a consensus had been reached on the subject, with further, logical elaborations.

---

2 Ibn Khaldun, *The Muqaddimah*, p. 389.
3 Commentary titled *Al-Qawl al-Mufīd 'ala ar-Risāla al-Musāma'a Wasīlat al-'Abīd fī 'Ilm at-Tawḥīd* ["Useful Remarks on the Work entitled 'Means of Devotion in the Science of Divine Unity'", c. 1908].

The Status of the Caliphate

5. We need, however, to elucidate the true meaning of several verses in the Qur'an with a view to eliminating any ambiguity about their potential bearing on the question of the imamate:

> *O believers, obey God and obey the Prophet and those set in authority over you. If you dispute among yourselves over any matter, refer it to God and the Messenger, if you believe in God and the Last Day. This would be best, and best also in consequence.*[4]

> *When there comes to them a report, bearing news of security or of foreboding, they spread it wide. Were they to refer it to the Messenger and to those set in authority over them, its true import would be ascertained from them by those best fitted to understand it. Were it not for God's bounty upon you and His mercy, you would have followed Satan, all but a few.*[5]

We do not know of any scholar who claims to find support in these verses for either of the two proposals in question. Therefore, in an effort to avoid being derailed by superfluous issues and arguments, we will not prolong this discussion.

Nevertheless, it should be noted that exegetes of the Qur'an interpreted the expression "those in authority" in the first of the verses quoted above as a reference to Muslim princes during the Prophet's lifetime as well as afterwards. These included caliphs, judges, military commanders and, according to the words of the Qur'an, "those in authority among them, those of them whose task it is to investigate", including theologians.[6]

Alternatively, the expression "those in authority" in the second verse refers to "the most acute-minded among the companions of the Prophet, or to those who were in authority among them".[7]

In either case, there is nothing in these two verses to support the argument in favour of the caliphate. At most, these verses may be interpreted to imply that certain people present, among Muslims, are entrusted with the conduct of their public affairs. This, of course, has a much wider, more general meaning than the

---

4 Qur'an 4.59.
5 Qur'an 4.83.
6 See the commentary by Al-Baydawi, *Ṭawāliʿ al-Anwār min Maṭāliʿ al-Anẓār* ["Manifestations from the Perspectives of the Horizon", c. 1300].
7 See al-Zamakhshari, *Al-Kashāf al-Tanzil* ["The Revealer", c. 1142].

Islam and the Foundations of Political Power

theory of the caliphate mentioned (by the religious scholars). The two differ to such an extent as to appear unrelated.

If one wished to enquire further into this topic one could consult the volume *The Caliphate* by the great scholar Sir Thomas Arnold.[8] The explanation offered in the second and third chapters of his work is both charming and persuasive.

It would be appropriate in this connection to cite the remark made by the author of the Mawāqif at the end of his argument about the need for the appointment of an imam through a consensus among Muslims:

> If it is claimed that the ijmā needs to be supported and if the supporting tradition were at hand, it would have been transmitted without interruption. For this would have been required. Either the consensus was that it was not considered necessary or, alternatively, that the support required would be by way of observable facts available only to the contemporaries of the Prophet.*

As is clear, this author concluded that the consensus in this connection was not verifiable. Moreover, the author of the Mawāqif would have had no reason to resort to such arguments if he had found support for this claim in the holy book.

If we read the Qur'an from beginning to end, we find the treatment of every possible case and details concerning all aspects of religion – *We have not neglected any matter in this Book*.[9] However, we do not find any reference to a general imamate or caliphate. This, then, is something that merits examination.

6. The issue of the caliphate is not only passed over in the Qur'an, it is equally ignored in the sunna. This is borne out by the fact that the religious scholars were unable to provide even a single hadith in support of their case on this issue. Had they found the least evidence to buttress their argument in the sunna, they would have used it to reinforce the idea of unanimous agreement. Had this been the case, the author of the *Mawāqif* would not have argued that the idea of unanimous agreement was not embedded in tradition.

7. Muhammad Rashid Rida, seeking to find evidence for the caliphate in the

---

* See Abdurrahman al-Eiji, *Al-Mawāqif fī-'ilm al-Kalām* ["Doctrines of Theology", 1355].
8 Sir Thomas Arnold, *The Caliphate* [Oxford, 1924].
9 Qur'an 6.38.

prophet's traditions, repeated the arguments used by Sa'ad al-Din Al Taftazani[10] in favour of this theory in his work *Al Maqāṣid*. However, none of the arguments used in the *Al Maqāṣid* were to be found in the Qur'an or the sunna. Rida therefore accused Sa'ad al-Din of having "neglected", just like the other authors, to back up his conclusion regarding the need for the appointment of an imam. These hadiths are explicit about the collective commitment of Muslims towards their imams, and in some cases go as far as to state that anyone who dies without having sworn allegiance to an imam dies the death of a jahili.* Likewise, in the authenticated hadith transmitted by Hodayfa, the prophet speaks of "a binding obligation for the whole community of Muslims and their imam".[11]

Before considering this objection, we should note that the author admits what we have already pointed out, namely, that the claims of the religious scholars lack support in the sunna.

In fact, Rida's contribution to this debate was not novel. Ibn Hazm[12] had already said: "Both the Qur'an and the sunna lay down the obligation to obey the imam, as is made clear by the verse: 'O you who have attained to faith! Pay heed unto God and pay heed unto the Apostle and unto those from among you who have been entrusted with authority',[13] and by many other genuine hadiths of the Prophet which stress the obligation to institute the imamate and obey the imams."[14]**

However, when we examine these words of the Prophet, we find nothing more than allusions to notions such as the "imamate", "allegiance", "community" and so on. This is the case for instance in the following hadiths:

> The imams should be of Qurayshi origin; it is binding upon the community of Muslims; the person who dies without having sworn allegiance to an

---

* This notion is conventionally used to indicate one who has not been enlightened by the faith; however, etymologically it would be translated as "pagan" or "savage" in the sense of one who has not yet been "civilised".

** Abdel Razek uses the word "imam" according to one of its two main meanings in the Sunni lexicon, rendering it interchangeable with "caliph"; he does not take into account the various Shi'a meanings and associations with the concept of "imama".

10 Sa'ad al-Din Al Taftazani, Mas'ud ibn 'Umar or 'Umar ibn Mas'ud, born in Taftazan (a locality in Khorassan) in 722 AH [1322], died in Samarkand in 792 AH [1390]. [See *Al-Fawā'id al-Bahīya fi Tarājim al-Ḥanafīya* ["The Splendid Benefits of Hanafi Biographies"], c. 1357.]
11 Muhammad Rashid Rida, *Al-Khilāfa wal-Imāma al-'Uẓma* ["The Caliphate and the Great Imamate", 1924].
12 Abu Muhammad 'Ali ibn Ahmad ibn Said, born in Cordoba in 384 AH [994] and died in 456 AH [1063].
13 Qur'an 4.59.
14 Ibn Hazm, *Al-Faṣl fil-Milal wal-Niḥal* ["The Book of Sects and Creeds", c. 994–1064].

imam is like someone who dies without having adhered to Islam; if someone has given allegiance to an imam and committed his actions and sentiments to him, he is bound to obey him as far as possible; if someone disputes the imam's authority, he should be decapitated; and follow the example of those who come after me – Abu Bakr, 'Umar, and so on.[15]

Nothing in the above quotation supports the claim that the sharī'a conclusively lays down the principle of the caliphate or the great imamate, understood as a deputyship for the Prophet and a fulfilment of the functions that he undertook among Muslims.

We do not wish to question the authenticity of the hadiths drawn upon here, although there might be a lot to say on that issue. Let us assume, for the sake of discussion, that all the hadiths are authentic. Nor do we wish to debate the significance given by the Lawgiver (the Prophet Muhammad) to the words "imamate", "allegiance", "community" and so on.

We would embark on a discussion of the significance of these words if we wanted to illustrate that these expressions, as used in the religious law, do not carry the same interpretations as those introduced later, in Islamic discourse, after the fact.

We will, however, disregard these above-mentioned controversial questions and assume that all the afore-mentioned hadiths are authentic, that the notions of "imam" and "caliph" carry the same meaning in the sharī'a as they do for contemporary supporters of the "great imamate"; that "allegiance" refers to allegiance to the caliph; and that "Muslim community" and the community governed by the Islamic caliphate mean the same thing.

Even upon accepting all of the above premises, and admitting all possible concessions; we cannot find, in the entire body of the above-cited traditions, any evidence that the institution of the caliphate is a matter of religious dogma, or that it is entailed by religious belief.

Jesus Christ said, "render unto Caesar what is Caesar's".* This Biblical phrase does not mean that Jesus attributed a divine foundation to Caesar's government. It does not decree that recognition of Caesar's government is a part of the Christian creed. No one who has an understanding of linguistic usage can interpret Jesus' words in a manner that would support assumptions of this sort.

---

* Matthew 22.21.

15 These hadiths are quoted in Rashid Rida, *Al-Khilāfa wal-Imāma al-'Uẓma* ["The Caliphate and the Great Imamate", 1924].

The Status of the Caliphate

The above allusions to the concepts of "caliphate", "imamate" and "allegiance" in the Prophet's hadiths do not mean anything beyond what Christ meant when he referred to the legal requirements pertaining to the government of Caesar.

If it is true that the Prophet commanded us to obey an imam whom we ourselves have nominated, then it is no less true that God has commanded us to honour our agreements with polytheists and to be fair in our dealings with them as long as they are fair to us. This does not mean that God sanctions polytheism, or that we should, in compliance with His order, sanction it ourselves. Does the religious law not require us to obey tyrants and unjust rulers if we are obliged to do so and if we reckoned that acting otherwise would cause grave unrest? Such a precept does not mean that tyranny is legitimate, or that rebellion against a government is lawful. Are we not commanded by the shari'a to be generous to beggars, considerate to the poor, and kind and compassionate towards them? Would a reasonable man deduce from this that we should make it a point to have poor people and beggars in our midst?

Again, God talks to us about slavery. He exhorts us to set slaves free, to treat them well and lays down several other recommendations regarding them. However, this does not imply that slavery is a religious obligation, or that it is desirable.

The same applies to issues such as divorce, borrowing, commerce, mortgaging and so on, mentioned frequently in God's book and plainly regulated in His law. This does not mean that these issues are religious duties, or that they have a special significance for God.

It is now easy to see what conclusion may be drawn from the fact that the Prophet spoke about issues such as the covenant of allegiance, power, government and obedience to those in authority; even promulgating rules in this regard.

To treat the caliphate as a requirement of religious law is a proposition that has consequences of great magnitude. To resort to hadiths, even hadiths of proven authenticity, in an effort to legitimise this point of view, does not take the gravity of such a proposition fully into account.

3
The Caliphate from the Social Point of View

The claim regarding consensus [ijmā] – An examination of this claim – The decline of political science amongst Muslims – Muslim interest in Greek learning – Uprisings among Muslims against the caliphate – The caliph's reliance on coercion and suppression – Islam as a religion of human equality and honour – The office of the caliphate as a focus of affection and fervour – The caliphate, autocracy and oppression – The ultimate argument in favour of the caliphate – Caliphal royal resistance to a revival of the intellectual and political sciences – A rejection of the doctrine of consensus – Religion recognises the institution of government – Government is not synonymous with the caliphate – The need for political authority, regardless of what type – The caliphate is not required by either religious or worldly criteria – The end of the caliphate in Islam – The nominal caliphate in Egypt – The outcome

1. For want of evidence from the Qur'an and the sunna, it was maintained that:

   After the Prophet's death, there was ongoing consensus among the Muslims during the first era of Islam to ensure that the position of the imam did not fall vacant. In point of fact, Abu Bakr, in his famous address after the Prophet's death, declared that the situation warranted someone to serve as a custodian of the faith. Everyone was united in entrusting to Abu Bakr the organisation of what was at that moment the most important task, namely, the burial of the Prophet. From that time on, in every age, Muslims acted likewise to nominate an imam to administer their affairs.[1]

---

[1] See Al-Eiji (d. 1355), *Al-Mawāqif fī-'ilm al-Kalām* ["Doctrines in Theology"], 1355 and related commentaries in the same.

Islam and the Foundations of Political Power

2. Setting aside any possible disagreements, let us assume the legitimacy of ijmā.[2] Let us assume too, that consensus is capable of being secured in practice,[3] and thereby ignore the objections of those who argue to the contrary and insist that this is not so. Nevertheless, we are of the opinion that the argument for consensus in this matter is quite unreliable. The authors we have discussed seem to find it impossible to produce evidence in support of their thesis. In any case, we will try to show that the reference to ijmā is unjustifiable as well as inaccurate; whether it involves the companions of the Prophet, or whether along with the companions it also includes the second generation of Muslims, or even the entire body of Muslim theologians.

3. The history of Muslim intellectual life shows that in comparison with other branches of learning, political science was notably neglected. It occupied a very modest position among other disciplines. Muslim intellectual activity displays a distinct absence of inquiry into systems of government or the foundations of political life. Minor endeavours, which are narrow in scope, do exist, but viewed in the context of the total intellectual output, these isolated exceptions seem all too limited and we do not find a single author or translator who specialises in the subject. Paradoxically, there were many valid reasons for Muslims to pursue serious research in political science, as a number of factors in their circumstances would motivate an earnest engagement with such an enquiry.

4. At the very least, the passion with which Muslims had taken to Greek science and philosophy should have served as a source of interest in the area of political science; given the natural intelligence and insatiable scientific curiosity to which this testified. The works of the Greeks that were studied and translated by Muslims had the potential to encourage them to investigate this subject. Political science is a very old discipline indeed. It had attracted interest among the

---

2 [The claim here is] that ijmā constitutes a formal legitimacy that is recognised as such by the majority of the community, with the exception only of those who followed differing views such as Ibrahim al-Nazzam the Mu'tazilite, al-Qashani and most of the Rafidites [rejectionists]. See Adbul-Aziz al-Bukhari, *Kashf al-Asrār* ["The Unveiling of Secrets", c. 800].
3 Some Rafidites and the Mu'tazilite al-Nazzam reject the possibility that ijmā can occur regarding matters that are not essential. Daoud and his partisans among the Zahirites and, following a few witnesses, Ibn-Hanbal, claimed that ijmā would only prevail among the Prophet's Companions. The Zaydis and the Shi'a imams support the idea that ijmā can be valid only if it is authorised by the progeny of the Prophet (descendants of Imam 'Ali). Malik ibn Anas is said to have held that ijmā was valid only among the people of Medina. See Adbul-Aziz al-Bukhari, *Kashf al-Asrār* ["The Unveiling of Secrets", c. 800].

The Caliphate from the Social Point of View

forerunners of Greek philosophy and had left a deep imprint on their intellectual production, indeed, on their very lives.

5. There was another more pertinent incentive for Muslims to study political science. From the appointment of Abu Bakr as first caliph to our own day, the institution of the caliphate has never ceased to provoke uprisings. It has never been free of challenges, to the extent that there is not a single caliph in Muslim history who has not encountered opposition, or a single generation that did not witness the assassination of the incumbent of this office.

Now, this is undoubtedly true of all absolutist regimes, regardless of the nationality, faith or time period in question. We are convinced, however, that the Muslim case is unique in this respect, and it does not allow for comparison with other nations. The chronicles of Muslim history clearly indicate that from its very inception, the seat of the caliph has always faced opposition.

The history of this opposition has been momentous and is thus of tremendous significance to note. At certain times, the opposition was a strong, well-organised and blatant force. This was the case with the Kharijites under 'Ali ibn Abi Talib.* At other times, it proceeded in a more clandestine manner, under the guise of esoteric systems such as the *Batiniyya*.** This was the case with the "partisans of union and progress".† At times an opposition movement would atrophy, becoming nearly extinct, while at others, it would flourish enough to shake the thrones of rulers. Sometimes, a movement engaged in vigorous action, while on other occasions, it would resort to tactics such as theological and religious propaganda.

---

* c. 596–661. 'Ali ibn Abi Talib (known as Ali) was the cousin and son-in-law of the Prophet Muhammad and the fourth caliph after the Prophet's death in 632. The Shi'a believe that Muhammad chose Ali as his successor and that Ali therefore should have become caliph following Muhammad's death. But Sunni Muslims consider Ali as the fourth and final of the rightly guided caliphs. This disagreement split the umma into its two branches of Sunni and Shi'a.

** *Batin* in Arabic means "hidden" or "implicit". Its opposite is *zahir* or *dhahir*, that is, explicit or visible. For some Muslim communities, Qur'anic verses have an inner, or implicit (some contemporary interpreters say "esoteric"), meaning alongside the explicit, apparent, accessible-to-all meaning. For Shi'a communities, it is the imam who can access the hidden meaning and can derive guidance from it for the benefit of their communities. For Sufis, the initiated (*shaykh*) would fulfil this function to some degree. In late usage within Sunni circles, the Batiniyya, that is, adepts of the batin, came to refer to some Shi'a communities in particular (Ismailis and Alevis), who are considered to have freely interpreted verses of the Qur'an and derived from them views that stand beyond "orthodoxy". In some Sunni usage, this has tainted the term with a pejorative tone. Here, Abdel Razek has adopted this term as used by Sunni theologians, that is, as a category that refers to particular Shi'a communities

† Abdel Razek is alluding to the movement initiated by reformists in the Ottoman Empire during the early twentieth century.

Islam and the Foundations of Political Power

The protagonists of these movements could well have pursued systematic enquiry into the phenomenon of political power and delved into an analysis of its origins. They could have examined governments and the conditions that influence them. They could have investigated the caliphate and its foundations critically, addressing the themes that relate to political science. It is undeniable, that of all peoples, the Arabs had the most cogent reasons to be interested in political science and to encourage those who were engaged in this branch of learning.

6. Why, then, did they retreat from these investigations? Why did they neglect to study Plato's *Republic* and Aristotle's *Politics*, even as they admired the latter to the point of calling him the "First Teacher"? Why were the Muslim masses kept in total ignorance of the principles of politics and of the different kinds of governments invented by the Greeks; while they were all too willing to teach them the methods of the Assyrians in grammar and to train them in the discipline of mathematics that the Indian author, Baidaba, mentions in the *Kalilah wa Dimnah*.* They prevented this, even as they were willing to assimilate their religious disciplines with those of Greek philosophy to explore varying notions and ideas of right and wrong, belief and unbelief.

The scholars did not neglect political science because they were ignorant of it or because they were unaware of its importance. The reason for this patent neglect lies elsewhere, as we shall see below.

The origin of the caliphate is that it be "referred to the choice of those who pledge and un-pledged their allegiance", since "the imamate is a pledge which functions through those who pledge and un-pledge their allegiance to the one whom they chose, having consulted among themselves, to be the leader of the community and the imam of the umma".[4]

This might imply that the institution of the caliphate is based on voluntary allegiance and that it relies on appointment by the will of those who pledge and un-pledge their allegiance. It is conceivable that an institution of this nature could have existed. However, if we examine how events really came to pass, we find that the caliphate was founded not on voluntary allegiance but rather by sheer

---

* Translated from the Persian into Arabic by Ibn al-Muqaffa (d. c. 756), *Kalilah wa Dimnah* is a collection of animal fables based on tales translated through Syriac from old Indian sources. It became a great classic of Arabic literature and has been translated into many European languages, thus the collection has many different titles. See Ramsay Wood, *Kalila and Dimna: Fables of Friendship and Betrayal*, London: Saqi Books, 2008.

4 Rashid Rida, *Al-Khilāfa wal-Imāma al-'Uẓma* ["The Caliphate and the Great Imamate", 1924].

coercion, and that in most instances this took the form of a physical, military coercion. The caliph had only arrows and swords for his defence. He relied upon well-armed, intrepid armies. Without these he could not have maintained his position or been able to rule.

It may be difficult for us to acknowledge that the first three orthodox caliphs relied on physical force to establish their authority and maintained it by recourse to suppression and coercion. However, can we doubt that both 'Ali and Mu'awiyya, the fourth and fifth caliphs, rose to the caliphate by means of the sword and that this trend persisted without change during subsequent eras, down to the present day. There was no way that the "Prince of the Believers" [*amir al-mu'minin*], the Sultan of Turkey, Mehmet VI,[5] could have resided in Yeldiz, had he not been constantly surrounded by armies to guard his residence and to face death whilst safeguarding his throne and his very life.

We have no doubt that coercion has always been the basis of the caliphate. History does not offer us a single example of a caliph whose image is not associated with the fear inspired by the brutal force surrounding him, with the armed force supporting him, and the unsheathed swords that lent him protection.

If it were not for the risk of pushing our discourse beyond acceptable limits, we would have presented evidence of repression and coercion with regard to every caliph down to our time, so that it would become plain to the reader that the throne has been erected on the heads of soldiers and carried upon their necks. Crowns are preserved only at the expense of human lives. The power of rulers is upheld by destroying the power of humankind. Their pomp and grandeur is fed by extortions from people, just as night thrives at the expense of day and shortens it. Their light springs from the glimmer of swords and flames, ignited in wars.

During certain historical moments, this armed force that upholds the caliphate is less visible and therefore not perceived by the populace. This is not an exception to the conclusion that we have outlined above. While it is possible that during certain periods of time force would not be used due to a lack of need for it, the armed forces have been imperative in supporting the rank of the caliph. During these more passive phases, people would tend to disregard the presence of the armed forces and sometimes forget that it existed. However, if this force was not continually present, then the caliphate could not have continued to subsist. As Ibn Khaldun has attested: "Royal authority means

---

5 We wrote this at a time when the caliphate was still in place in Turkey. Mehmet VI [1861–1926], reigning from 1918 to 1922] was caliph, until such a time as he lost the effective power that, as mentioned above, lies at the foundation of the caliphate.

superiority and the power to rule by force; kingship is nothing but coercion and rule by constraint".⁶ Anushivan says in the same vein that, "kingship relies upon soldiers" and Aristotle has also declared that kingship is a regime supported by the soldiery.*

7. Naturally, autocracy cannot be established in any nation, except through domination and suppression. Moreover, it is also natural that this should be the case with Muslims more so than with any other community. For, Islam did not satisfy itself with merely teaching its followers the ideals of fraternity and equality; that human beings are equal to one another like the teeth of a comb; that their slaves are in fact their brethren in faith and that the faithful must support each other. No! The message of Islam did not confine itself to a theoretical and abstract teaching of these principles. On the contrary, it taught the faithful to abide by these principles in their daily lives and to uphold these values in their activities. It established laws founded upon the principles of fraternity and equality, put them to test in real circumstances and gave Muslims a concrete sense of these principles. Their trustworthy Prophet did not depart from them until he had stamped the new faith on their hearts and infused its doctrines into their souls. Their polity came into its own only when anyone among the faithful could address the caliph from across his rostrum and declare: "Had we noticed any transgression on your part, we would have redressed it with our swords."

It is natural that these Muslims would believe in freedom as a principle and that they would adopt its ways in practice. These early Muslims believed in freedom the way they believed in their religion. They cherished it in their everyday lives, refusing to submit to anyone other than God, whom they addressed directly, as their faith had taught them to do, during the five prayers of the day. It came naturally to these self-respecting men to resist the subjugation demanded by kings. They submitted only under duress or the threat of the sword. Consequently, as we have pointed out, the caliphate could only have been consolidated by means of force. With the exception of certain specific occasions, this "force" took the shape of a physical army.

We are not especially interested in understanding every aspect of the issue at hand. It may be as discussed above, or there may have been additional circumstances which have not been examined here. What is important for us to

---

* See Aristotle's *Politics*, trans. T. A. Sinclair, rev. T. J. Saunders, London: Penguin Classics, 1981.
6 Ibn Khaldun, *The Muqaddimah*, p. 284.

The Caliphate from the Social Point of View

coercion, and that in most instances this took the form of a physical, military coercion. The caliph had only arrows and swords for his defence. He relied upon well-armed, intrepid armies. Without these he could not have maintained his position or been able to rule.

It may be difficult for us to acknowledge that the first three orthodox caliphs relied on physical force to establish their authority and maintained it by recourse to suppression and coercion. However, can we doubt that both 'Ali and Mu'awiyya, the fourth and fifth caliphs, rose to the caliphate by means of the sword and that this trend persisted without change during subsequent eras, down to the present day. There was no way that the "Prince of the Believers" [*amir al-mu'minin*], the Sultan of Turkey, Mehmet VI,[5] could have resided in Yeldiz, had he not been constantly surrounded by armies to guard his residence and to face death whilst safeguarding his throne and his very life.

We have no doubt that coercion has always been the basis of the caliphate. History does not offer us a single example of a caliph whose image is not associated with the fear inspired by the brutal force surrounding him, with the armed force supporting him, and the unsheathed swords that lent him protection.

If it were not for the risk of pushing our discourse beyond acceptable limits, we would have presented evidence of repression and coercion with regard to every caliph down to our time, so that it would become plain to the reader that the throne has been erected on the heads of soldiers and carried upon their necks. Crowns are preserved only at the expense of human lives. The power of rulers is upheld by destroying the power of humankind. Their pomp and grandeur is fed by extortions from people, just as night thrives at the expense of day and shortens it. Their light springs from the glimmer of swords and flames, ignited in wars.

During certain historical moments, this armed force that upholds the caliphate is less visible and therefore not perceived by the populace. This is not an exception to the conclusion that we have outlined above. While it is possible that during certain periods of time force would not be used due to a lack of need for it, the armed forces have been imperative in supporting the rank of the caliph. During these more passive phases, people would tend to disregard the presence of the armed forces and sometimes forget that it existed. However, if this force was not continually present, then the caliphate could not have continued to subsist. As Ibn Khaldun has attested: "Royal authority means

---

5 We wrote this at a time when the caliphate was still in place in Turkey. Mehmet VI [1861–1926], reigning from 1918 to 1922] was caliph, until such a time as he lost the effective power that, as mentioned above, lies at the foundation of the caliphate.

superiority and the power to rule by force; kingship is nothing but coercion and rule by constraint".[6] Anushivan says in the same vein that, "kingship relies upon soldiers" and Aristotle has also declared that kingship is a regime supported by the soldiery.*

7. Naturally, autocracy cannot be established in any nation, except through domination and suppression. Moreover, it is also natural that this should be the case with Muslims more so than with any other community. For, Islam did not satisfy itself with merely teaching its followers the ideals of fraternity and equality; that human beings are equal to one another like the teeth of a comb; that their slaves are in fact their brethren in faith and that the faithful must support each other. No! The message of Islam did not confine itself to a theoretical and abstract teaching of these principles. On the contrary, it taught the faithful to abide by these principles in their daily lives and to uphold these values in their activities. It established laws founded upon the principles of fraternity and equality, put them to test in real circumstances and gave Muslims a concrete sense of these principles. Their trustworthy Prophet did not depart from them until he had stamped the new faith on their hearts and infused its doctrines into their souls. Their polity came into its own only when anyone among the faithful could address the caliph from across his rostrum and declare: "Had we noticed any transgression on your part, we would have redressed it with our swords."

It is natural that these Muslims would believe in freedom as a principle and that they would adopt its ways in practice. These early Muslims believed in freedom the way they believed in their religion. They cherished it in their everyday lives, refusing to submit to anyone other than God, whom they addressed directly, as their faith had taught them to do, during the five prayers of the day. It came naturally to these self-respecting men to resist the subjugation demanded by kings. They submitted only under duress or the threat of the sword. Consequently, as we have pointed out, the caliphate could only have been consolidated by means of force. With the exception of certain specific occasions, this "force" took the shape of a physical army.

We are not especially interested in understanding every aspect of the issue at hand. It may be as discussed above, or there may have been additional circumstances which have not been examined here. What is important for us to

---

* See Aristotle's *Politics*, trans. T. A. Sinclair, rev. T. J. Saunders, London: Penguin Classics, 1981.
6 Ibn Khaldun, *The Muqaddimah*, p. 284.

illustrate is that the link between the caliphate and the use of violence is incontestable. Once established as a fact, it matters very little whether it conforms to principles of reason or follows religious rules.

To say that the caliphate is founded on suppression and force implies that these means are used to stifle any challenge to the caliph's office, any attack on his throne or its foundations. This is illustrated in the circumstances of Yazid's nomination, where a supporter gave a short, but highly charged speech. Pointing to Mu'awiyya, Yazid's father, he said: "This is the prince of the believers"; next, pointing to Yazid he said: "when he dies, it will be him"; finally, showing his sword, he cried: "and for those who object, it will be this".[7]

8. Whatever is secured and maintained by the sword becomes a prized possession. One is not likely to encourage or to give up anything that compromises this possession. Is this not especially true with matters of sovereignty and power? The human mind cherishes power even if it is obtained by means other than violence. When power is obtained by force and subjugation, the mind is all the more attached to it, all the more determined to defend it. One is apt to defend it more jealously than one might defend money, honour or women; and to love it more than all the riches of the world.

9. If there is anything that has ever driven men to despotism, injustice, aggression and iniquity, it is the desire for the position of caliph. We have seen how it has stirred up the most burning ambitions and the most violent, destructive forms of jealousy. When inordinate desire and destructive envy are brought together, and when they unite and find at their disposal the means for coercion, this can only lead to oppression and violence.

However, we must not confine ourselves to general principles and abstract theories. Let us return instead to indelible, historical facts.

Why else, other than out of envy for the position of caliph and the urge to cling to it along with its substantial powers, did Yazid ibn Mu'awiyya so wantonly

---

7 Ibn 'Abd Rabbuh [860–940], *Al-'Iqd al-Farid* ["The Unique Necklace", c. 900]. We find the narrative following which Mu'awiya ibn Abi Sufyan [founder of the Umayyad dynasty] wanted, in 55 AH [674], to secure the appointment of his son Yazid as heir to the caliphate. With this in mind, he summoned representatives of all the provinces of his realm and received them whilst surrounded by his friends and allies. He then asked for their views regarding the eligibility of his son to inherit the caliphate. After a number of speakers, Yazid ibn al-Muqaffa' stood up and said while pointing at Mu'awiyya that "The prince of believers is this one ..." At this point, Mu'awiyya commended him and said: "Sit down, you are the best orator!"

Islam and the Foundations of Political Power

violate the noble blood of the Prophet's line in the personage of Husayn, son of Fatima, the daughter of God's messenger? Why else did Yazid attack Medina, the original capital of the caliphate, the erstwhile city of the Prophet?* Was it not ambition for the office of the caliph and a desire for power which drove 'Abd Al-Malik ibn-Marwan** to desecrate the holy places of Islam? Is it for nothing that Ibn Abbas has come to be known as bloodthirsty and was it not the blood of his fellow Muslims that he so wantonly shed? Were not the Umayyads whom he fought his own kinsmen?

We can cite countless examples in this vein. This was how the Abbasids massacred one another, as well as the descendants of Sabu. The saintly Najm al-Din al-Ayyubi, renowned for his moral uprightness, fought with his own brother, Abu Bakr ibn al-Kamil, deposing him and throwing him into jail. The Mamluk and Ottoman Circassian dynasties knew many cases of the destitution and assassination of kings. Needless to say, all this was a result of the lure of the office of the caliph and the aggrandising appetites it stirred up, along with the readily available physical force of the armies.

10. Attraction to the privileges of royal power incites kings to defend their thrones against whatever might threaten their foundations and detract from their aura of sanctity. It follows, therefore, that they behave like wild beasts towards men who defy them or attack their position. It also follows that they should oppose intellectual enquiry, even of the most scientific kind, if they suspect that it constitutes a threat, however uncertain.

This is the reason why rulers have opposed enquiry and subjected educational institutions to censorship whenever possible. Certainly, political science, inasmuch as it seeks to understand the nature, specifics and structure of different forms of government, poses an especially strong threat to those in power. It is normal, then, for rulers to oppose it on principle and to try their utmost to stop people from pursuing a study of it.

This is how we might explain the all too obvious weakness of the political

---

* Abdel Razek is alluding to the battle of al-Hurra, which saw an army sent by Yazid to fight the people of Medina who had proclaimed Abdullah ibn al-Zubayr as caliph. The army was led by Muslim ibn 'Uqbah and included a large number of Syrian Christians. The battle ended with an invasion and ransacking of Medina on 26 August 673. See Philip K. Hitti, *History of the Arabs*, rev. 10th edn, New York: Palgrave Macmillan, 2002.

** The allusion here is to the siege of Mecca during the reign of the Umayyad caliph Abd al-Malik ibn Marwan. Led by Al-Hajjaj ibn Yusuf al-Thaqafi, the siege began on 25 March 692 and lasted for seven months. It ended with the bombardment of the city and its inhabitants with rocks and was followed by the defeat and assassination of Ibn al-Zubayr.

The Caliphate from the Social Point of View

sciences in Muslim history and the neglect of inquiry into this area in the intellectual endeavours of Muslims. It also explains the failure of Muslims to treat these questions in a manner commensurate with their abilities and their attainments in other domains of knowledge.

11. It is no wonder, then, that the achievements of Muslims in political science should be so meagre and moribund. It is surprising in fact, that in view of the many hurdles mentioned above, this branch of knowledge was not altogether extinguished. We cannot but marvel at the fact that notwithstanding the enormous pressures and the ever-present threat of unrelenting repression, the world of learning included a few works on politics and a small number of intellectuals remained opposed to the point of view of the caliphs.

This book would have been ten times as long if it were to give a complete account of the opposition of Muslim monarchies to political expressions and political science. Short of this, we will confine ourselves to some brief indications, hoping that readers will go on to consult other works on this subject.

Let us return to the claim that the Muslim umma was unanimous on the principle of proclaiming an imam and that this unanimity makes such proclamation a duty.

Let us suppose that the umma had unanimously abstained from proclaiming an imam and that subsequently there had been unanimous agreement on the principle of abstention. Or, let us suppose to the contrary that the umma, in its entirety with all its constituents, had effectively participated at all times in allegiance to the system of the imamate; that it had thus formally recognised it; and that a plain and unambiguous ijmā had thus been realised. We would still be entitled to dispute this as a real instance of ijmā. We would be justified in drawing from it a juridical principle and turning it into a religious argument.

In the discussion of Yazid's[8] investiture, we saw how allegiance was extorted and the agreement of Muslims obtained. Yet other examples can be added to illustrate these points.

The case of Yazid brings to mind that of Faisal ibn Husayn ibn 'Ali. His father, Husayn ibn 'Ali, prince of Arabia, sided with the Allies in the First World War in revolt against the Turkish sultan who prided himself as the Caliph of the Muslims. His sons organised campaigns of support in different regions of Arabia for the battles of the allied forces against their Turkish and German enemies,

---

8 See Chapter 3, section 7.

among others. Faisal was highly esteemed by the English for his brave feats in their support and his exemplary steadfastness in their service. As a reward to him, the English designated him as the king of Syria. However, no sooner was he appointed than the French army expelled him. Faisal had to flee to England, renouncing his kingdom, surrendering his power and all that went with it. The English assigned him to Iraq, where they proclaimed him as king on the pretext that he had been pronounced as king by unanimous agreement with the exception only of a small group of influential individuals of the type Ibn Khaldun calls "deviants".

In fact, the English were correct. They had indeed organised elections, apparently in accordance with the principles of free and legitimate consultation. They had consulted several Iraqi notables. They duly "elected" Faisal. It was the same procedure through which the famous orator secured allegiance to Yazid. Can this be described as ijmā?

Even if this so-called ijmā had taken place, was it valid in these circumstances? Was it even an acceptable form of ijmā? And how can one bank on it considering, as previously mentioned, that the Kharijites and some of the Mu'tazilites, such as Al-Assamm, had denied that the proclamation of an imam was ever a religious duty? Thus, to refute the thesis that there was unanimous agreement on this issue, it will suffice to recall the opposition of Al-Assamm, the Mu'tazilites and the others. This opposition was real, even though Ibn Khaldun dismisses its protagonists as "deviants".

12. We have seen how the Holy Qur'an neither mentions the caliphate, nor alludes to it. It is ignored in the tradition of the Prophet and no ijmā ever pronounced it. To what other argument can the partisans of the caliphate take recourse? Can one still talk about a religious duty in the absence of any support for this thesis, be it in the sacred book, the tradition of the Prophet or by way of unanimous agreement on the part of the believers?

There remains one argument which our critics might deploy, though it is weak and shaky. It is the proposition that the caliphate is a necessary condition for the practice of religion and the realisation of the general good of the Muslim community.[9]

13. Specialists in public law acknowledge that the optimal functioning of any

---

9 See the argument offered on this point in Chapter 2, section 3.

The Caliphate from the Social Point of View

civilised society, whether it rests on a single religion, such as Islam, Christianity or Judaism, or whether it is multi-confessional, and, furthermore, whatever the race, colour or language of the people concerned may be, requires the presence of a government to keep order and manage its affairs. The forms and features of the government might, of course, vary: it may be constitutional or despotic, republican or Bolshevik, and so on. Scholars of public law disagree on what constitutes the best system. But none of them to our knowledge has ever disputed the need for a government, whatever its form, in every society. We do not need to reproduce their arguments in this regard. We do not, however, doubt that this argument is essentially correct. Abu Bakr, the first caliph, probably had no other consideration in mind but this when he said that "this religion (the community of believers) needs someone to take charge of its affairs". The Qur'an seems to be of this opinion too:

Is it they who hand out the mercy of your Lord?

We distributed their livelihoods among them in this present life, and raised some above others in rank, that some might take others into their service. But the mercy of your Lord is better than what they amass.[10]

So let those who follow the Evangel judge in accordance with what God revealed in it. Who so judges not in accordance with what God revealed, these are the dissolute.

To you We revealed the Book with the Truth, confirming previous Scripture and witnessing to their veracity. So judge between them as God revealed and do not follow their whims, to turn you away from the truth revealed to you.

For every community We decreed a law and a way of life. Had God willed, He could have made you a single community – but in order to test you in what He revealed to you. So vie with one another in virtue. To God is your homecoming, all of you, and He will then acquaint you with that over which you differed.

So judge between them as God revealed and do not follow their whims, and beware lest they tempt you away from certain things that God revealed to you. If they turn away in denial, know that God wishes to chastise them for some of their sins – many are the sinners among mankind! Do they truly desire the law of paganism? But who is fairer than God in judgement for a people firm of faith?

---

10 Qur'an 43.32.

O believers, take not Jews and Christians for allies; they are allies one of another. Who so among you takes them as allies is accounted of their number. God guides not the wrongdoers.[11]

14. We can safely assert, then, that like all other peoples, the Muslims, inasmuch as they form a distinct community, need a government to manage and organise their affairs.

If this is how theologians understand the caliphate, if they attribute to it the meaning that public law specialists give to the notion of government, we can say that they are right and join them in affirming that such an institution is indeed necessary for the conduct of religious practices and the quest for the public good. The caliphate would in this sense be the equivalent of a government which, whatever its form, whether it is personal or republican, despotic, constitutional, consensual, democratic, socialist, Bolshevik, etc., fits this definition. However, this argument does not allow us to proceed any further: we may not draw further inferences from this self-evident observation.

On the other hand, if by the caliphate the theologians mean the specific institution called by this name, then their argument is weak and the evidence inadequate.

15. Observation supported by reasoning and evidence from ancient and modern history show that the performance of religious rites as well as other aspects of religion do not necessitate the kind of government which theologians call the caliphate, nor do these require the presence of leaders known as caliphs. In fact, it should be noted that the temporal interests of Muslims do not depend on these arrangements either. Neither the conduct of our spiritual life, nor the direction of our temporal affairs calls for the caliphate.

To extend this analysis, the caliphate has always been, and still remains, a disaster for Islam and for Muslims. It has been a constant source of evil and corruption. We will elaborate on this point later. For the time being let us content ourselves with recalling the obvious considerations which show that our religion is not dependent, any more than our temporal affairs, on the "caliphate" of the theologians.

---

11 Qur'an 5.47–51.

The Caliphate from the Social Point of View

16. We have already mentioned Ibn Khaldun's remark[12] according to which: "The caliphate dissolved and its impact vanished when the Arabs lost their spirit of collective solidarity and when, in consequence, their momentum faded away and their strength had gone; then all that remained was pure kingship, with no relation whatsoever with the caliphate." Can we say this situation unhinged the foundation of the faith or compromised the interests of the community in a way which the caliphate (as might be claimed) would have helped prevent?

Since the middle of the third century of the hijra, the caliphate began losing the territories in its preserve, to the point, over time, when its influence was confined to the capital Baghdad. Thus:

> Khorasan and the regions situated beyond the Euphrates passed under the dominion of Ibn Saman. Under his descendants Bahrain passed to the Qarmatis, Yemen to Ibn Tabataba, Isfahan and Fars to the Buyids, Ahwaz and Wasit to Mu'izz al-Dawla, Aleppo to Saif al-Dawla, Egypt to Ahmad ibn Tulun and later to the rulers who gained control over it and founded independent kingdoms, like the Fatimids, the Ayyubids, the Mamluks and others.[13]

Religious principles were not adhered to any more in Baghdad than in the regions which broke away from it. Nor was the religion held in higher esteem there than anywhere else. Life in Baghdad was no better and the temporal affairs of Muslims were, if anything, in a worse condition.

17. The caliphate collapsed in Baghdad in the middle of the eighth century of the hijra, when the city was attacked by the Tartars. The Abbasid Caliph Al Mu'tassim Billah was slaughtered along with his family and officers of the state. The Muslim community remained without a caliph for three years.[14]

At this time Egypt was under the yoke of Zaher Bibars. With a calculated plan, this cunning ruler set out in search of a descendant of the Abbasids who might have escaped the massacre. By chance he found a man believed to be one of the last survivors of the dynasty. This discovery fitted with Zaher's plan and enabled him to restore a caliphal cell in Egypt entirely in his control. Thus, he installed a dynasty of figureheads whom he declared to be the "Caliphs of

---

12 See Chapter 1, section 7.
13 Jalal ad-Din as-Suyuti, *The History of the Khalifas Who Took the Right Way* [c. 1400].
14 Suyuti, *The History of the Khalifas Who Took the Right Way*.

Muslims", obliging the believers to honour them and yield to their ostensible authority, while in reality it was he who wielded power, manipulating the symbols associated with the caliphate as he pleased. The Seljuk kings turned this practice into a family tradition until, finally, the Ottoman sultans assumed the title of caliph in 923 AH [1517].

Muslim interests, whether spiritual or temporal, were never served by elevating impotent figureheads to rulers over Egypt. Despite being adorned with the title of caliph, these puppets served no good. What was the situation of the extensive realm of Islam beyond Egypt, where the shackles of the caliphate had been cast away, where its authority was disregarded, and whose inhabitants have lived, and still live, free from the shadow of the caliphs and their supposedly sacred glory? Were the practices of faith neglected there more than anywhere else? Did any single catastrophe befall them? Did the sky over their temporal realm cave in when the caliphal star vanished from it? Did the bounty of the sky and the earth disappear when the caliph was gone? None of this came to pass.

The Caliphs were gone. The world did not lament their death.
Neither the feasts, nor the Fridays have shied away!

18. By God, no! Would God, who has vowed that this religion should last forever, place its greatness at the mercy of a specific type of government, or attach its destiny to a special category of power-holders? Would He want the fortunes and misfortunes of the community of the faithful to be subject to the system of the caliphate, or to the will of the caliphs? God, in His great majesty, is much too determined to ensure the perpetuity of the faith, and too merciful to the faithful to inflict such a system on them.

We hope that we have succeeded in clearly showing that the caliphate or great imamate is an institution based neither on the precepts of religious faith nor on reason; and that all the justifications proposed along these lines crumble when we subject them to careful examination.

We must now try to answer the questions which arise in the mind of the reader. We must set out our own views on the nature and the origins of the caliphate. May God help and support us in this endeavour.

Book Two

Islam and Government

4
The System of Power at the Time of the Prophet

The Prophet's practice as a judge – Did the Prophet appoint judges? – Omar's practice as a judge – 'Ali's practice (in this respect) – The practice of Mu'ad and Abu Mussa – Problems in ascertaining judicial practice at the time of the Prophet – The absence of kingship during the time of the Prophet – The failure of historians to inquire into the system of the regime of the Prophet – Was the Prophet a king?

1. We have seen from our survey of the history of juridical authority at the time of the Prophet that the facts in this regard remain surrounded with confusion and ambiguity. It is not easy in these circumstances to acquire a clear idea or to give an account that satisfies the standards of critical research.

There is no doubt that juridical authority in the sense of arbitration and resolution of conflicts at the time of the Prophet resembled the way in which it had been exercised among the Arabs and among other peoples, long before the advent of Islam. We know that disputes were brought to the attention of the Prophet; that he agreed to consider the cases submitted to his attention and to pronounce a judgement. He said: "You ask me to settle your disputes. It is possible that one of you presents their case in a more tendentious way than others. If in consequence my judgement accords an advantage to that one, at the expense of the legitimate rights of their adversaries, they will have nothing to rejoice in. For, I will thereby have offered them a portion of hell. They should not take profit from it."[1]

---

[1] Al-Bukhari, Ṣaḥīḥ al-Bukhārī [c. 810]. [*Ṣaḥīḥ al-Bukhārī* is one of the six canonical hadith collections of Sunni Islam. Its full title translates as "The Abridged Collection of Authentic Hadith with Connected Chains Regarding Matters Pertaining to the Prophet, His Practices and His Times".]

Islam and the Foundations of Political Power

Similarly, we find many examples of how the Prophet resolved the issues brought before him in reliable historical reports. However, it is very difficult, indeed impossible, to deduce from these examples the general system of justice adopted by the Prophet. Indeed, what we know about the Prophet's practice does not allow us to form a clear idea of its actual operation or its concrete organisation – assuming that it was organised in the first place.

2. We noted that the circumstances concerning juridical practice at that time are ambiguous and obscure in every respect. Hence, it is not even possible to establish whether or not the Prophet had appointed individuals with the responsibilities of a judge.

Most theologians consider three of the Prophet's companions to have been charged with the functions of a judge during his lifetime.

According to some authors,[2] "the Prophet entrusted 'Umar ibn al-Khattab, 'Ali ibn Abi Talib and Mu'ad ibn Jabal with the functions of a judge". To these should be added Abu Mussa al-Ash'ari, who probably had the same responsibilities as Mu'ad ibn Jabal.

3. It would be rather surprising from a historical point of view, if 'Umar ibn al-Khattab carried out the functions of a judge during the lifetime of the Prophet. This account seems to be derived from another report: according to Tirmidhi in *The Book of Traditions*,[*] the third caliph 'Uthman ibn 'Affan proposed that Abdallah ibn 'Umar (son of 'Umar ibn al-Khattab) should be charged with the functions of a judge. The latter refused, impelling 'Uthman to ask: "Why are you unwilling to exercise this responsibility, although your father did so regularly?"

"My father," Abdallah answered, "was able, when faced with complicated cases, to consult the Prophet; the Prophet could in turn consult the archangel Gabriel. But as for me, I do not see whom I could consult in case I am faced with difficulties."[3]

4. As for 'Ali ibn Abi Talib, he was sent by the Prophet as a judge to Yemen while he was still a young man. According to Abu Da'ud, 'Ali has said in this connection:

---

[*] Abdel Razek is referring to *Al-Jāmi' al-Ṣahih*, also known as *Sunan al-Tirmidhī*, a major hadith collection by al-Tirmidhī (824–92).

[2] Rifā'a Rāfi' at-Ṭahṭāwī, *Nihāyat al-Ijāz fī Sīrat Sākin al-Ḥijāz* ["The Ultimate Summary of the Life of an Inhabitant from the Hijaz", 1876].

[3] *Ibid.*

The System of Power at the Time of the Prophet

The Prophet sent me to Yemen to judge while I was still young, and had no experience in judging. He assured me that God would guide my heart and aid me in my judgements. If any two people embroiled in a dispute were to come to me, my duty would be to suspend any judgement until I had listened equitably to both sides. In this way, I would be able to form a clear idea of the judgement to give. Since then I have been making judgements in this way and I have never doubted the judgements I have given.[4]

This account is also reproduced by Abu 'Amr ibn 'Abd Al Barr in his work *Al-Istī'āb*.* He states that that the Prophet told his companions: "The one person who has proved most competent in the responsibilities of a judge is 'Ali ibn Abi Talib."

Al-Bukhari[5] reports in this connection that before proceeding to Mecca on his farewell pilgrimage, the Prophet sent Khalid ibn al-Walid at the head of a group of his companions to Yemen, but then sent 'Ali ibn Abi Talib instead to collect the *khums*.[6]** While the Prophet was still in Mecca, 'Ali returned from Yemen with the proceeds of his mission.

According to 'Ali ibn Burnhan din Al Halabi,[7] the Prophet sent 'Ali at the head of a group of soldiers to Yemen. The entire region of Hamadan converted to Islam in one day and 'Ali wrote to the Prophet to inform him of this. On hearing the news, the Prophet prostrated himself, then rose, and said, "Peace be upon Hamadan!" Afterwards, all the inhabitants of Yemen converted to Islam massively. This is what happened with the first mission. A second group, with three hundred horsemen, was sent to the region of Madhaj in Yemen, with 'Ali ibn Abi Talib at its head. 'Ali conquered the region, collected the spoils of war and returned to join the Prophet on his farewell pilgrimage.

5. Mu'ad ibn Jabal, on his part, was sent by the Prophet as a judge to the province of Janad.[8] The Prophet charged him with the task of teaching the Qur'an and

---

* Ibn 'Abd al-Barr (Yusuf ibn Abdallah), *Al-Istī'āb fī Ma'rifat al-Aṣḥāb* ["The Comprehensive Book of Knowledge about the Companions", 1901].

** Khums literally means one-fifth or 20 per cent. In Muslim legal terminology, it refers to one-fifth of the portion of one's wealth which is given as *zakat* – an alms-giving ordained in the Qur'an as a means of purifying one's wealth.

4 Rifa'a al-Tahṭawī, *Nihāyat al-Ijāz fī Sīrat Sākin al-Ḥijāz* ["The Ultimate Summary of the Life of an Inhabitant from the Hijaz", 1876].
5 Al-Bukhari [810–70], *Ṣaḥīḥ al-Bukhārī*, vol. 4.
6 Ibid.
7 'Ali ibn Burhan Din al-Ḥalabi, *Al-Sīra al-Ḥalabīya*, vol. 3 ["A Biography of the Prophet", c. 1460–1549].
8 Al-Bukhari, *Ṣaḥīḥ al-Bukhārā*, vol. 4.

Islamic laws to the inhabitants of this area and to deliver justice among them. He also charged him, in the year 8 AH on the tenth day of Ramadan, with the collection of alms-tax from the governors of Yemen. Janad is said to be a town in Yemen.

Al-Bukhari reports the following hadiths concerning this matter:

> The Messenger of God sent Abu Musa and Mu'ad ibn Jabal to Yemen. They were each assigned distinct regions of activity, as Yemen was divided into two regions. The Prophet advised them to favour gentleness over violence, and incentives over threats ...
>
> According to Ibn Abbas, when the Messenger of God sent Mu'ad ibn Jabal to Yemen, he told him, "You are going to a people of the Book. When you are among them, invite them to vouch that there is no god but God, and that Muhammad is the Apostle of God. If they agree, tell them that God has prescribed to them five prayers through the day and night. If they respond, tell them that God has levied on them an alms-tax which will distribute some of the wealth of the rich to the poor. If they are receptive to all this, avoid interfering with whatever else they do. Fear the cry of the oppressed, for there is no barrier between them and God."[9]

In Ahmed Zayni Dahlan's biography of the Prophet, we find a similar account of these facts: "The Prophet sent Abu Musa Al Ash'ari and Mu'ad ibn Jabal to Yemen before the final pilgrimage, in the year 8, 9 or 10 of the hijra (according to different testimonies). Each of the two was in charge of a specific area. Mu'ad's jurisdiction was over the hilly region bordering on Aden and included the community of Janad, while Abu Mussa's jurisdiction was over the lower plains."[10]

According to Ahmad, Abu Da'ud, Tirmidhi and others, Al Harith ibn 'Amr, nephew of Al Mughira ibn Shu'ba, reported the following testimony of one of Mu'ad's companions:

> When the Prophet entrusted Mu'ad with a mission in Yemen he asked him, "How are you going to proceed if you find yourself obliged to render justice?"

---

9 Al-Bukhari, *Les traditions islamiques* [c. 810, trans. Octave Houdas and William Marçais, 4 vols, Paris: Ernest Leroux, 1903–14].

10 See the biography [*sira*] of the Prophet published in parallel with that by al-Halabi, *As-Sira al-Ḥalabīya*. [Abdel Razek is referring to Ahmed Zayni Dahlan's biography of the Prophet, *As-Sira an-Nabawīya wal-Athār al-Muḥammadīya* ["A Biography of the Prophet and Muhammadan Traditions"], c. 1886.]

The System of Power at the Time of the Prophet

Mu'ad said, "I will refer to the Book of God."
The Prophet asked, "What if you do not find anything there?"
Mu'ad said, "I will refer to the Traditions of the Messenger of God."
The Prophet asked, "And what if you do not find anything, either in the Book of God or in the Traditions of his Messenger?"
Mu'ad answered, "In that case I will reach a judgement by my own means [ijtihad]. I will never give up!"
The Prophet then tapped him on his breast and said, "Praise be to God who has guided the agent of the Messenger of God along the same way as that of His Messenger."[11]

6. These varied accounts from which we have quoted show that we are right in concluding that it is difficult to know what judicial practice was like at the time of the Prophet. We can see this in the differing versions of the same event. 'Ali's mission to Yemen is sometimes presented as being that of a judge and at other times for purposes of collecting the alms-tax. The same is true for Mu'ad, who in one account is a judge, in another a general making conquests, and in yet a third account an instructor in the tenets of the new faith.

The author of the *As-Sīra al-Ḥalabīya* [al-Halabi] reports the different views on the nature of the responsibilities entrusted to Mu'ad. According to Ibn 'Abd Al Barr, Mu'ad was a judge. Al-Ghassani thinks he was a treasurer. Ibn Maymun's account leads one to think that Mu'ad was rather an official in charge of the prayers. This latter suggestion leads one to think that he had held the post of a governor.[12]

7. For a thorough study of the state of juridical authority at the time of the Prophet, and for a careful analysis and correct appraisal of all the information and accounts that have come down to us on this subject, we need to extend the scope of our inquiry to the system of government in Islam and its overall organisation at this time, as well as the procedures of management followed in the Islamic kingdom – that is, if the territories over which God had enabled His Prophet to exercise dominion could be called an empire or kingdom.

---

11 Reported by al-Shawkani [1759–1834], in his *Irshād al-Fuḥūl ila Taḥqīq al-Ḥaqq min 'Ilm al-'Uṣūl* ["The Master's Guidance in Achieving Truth from the Roots of Law (science of al-Uṣūl)", c. 1759–1834]. In this report, the author mentions that the chain of transmitters for this hadith is long, but it is generally accepted that this does not hinder its authenticity.
12 See the biography of the Prophet by M. Ahmed Zayni Dahlan [*As-Sīra an-Nabawīya wal-Athār al-Muḥammadīya* ["A Biography of the Prophet and Muhammadan Traditions", c. 1886].

Islam and the Foundations of Political Power

On inquiring into the judicial system of the times, we realise that neither this nor the other institutions and practices typical of any government existed in a clear or unequivocal shape during the lifetime of the Prophet. An objective scholar can conclude from this that the Prophet never in fact appointed a governor to keep order and administer the affairs in territories which God placed at his command. Everything that has been reported on this subject leads us to the conclusion that the Prophet from time to time delegated certain limited functions, such as command over troops, supervision of property, leadership of the prayer, instruction in the Qur'an, and the propagation of the faith, to certain individuals. These assignments were not continuous or permanent, as we can see from examples of pronouncements during military missions or expeditions; as well as from the examples of appointing a deputy during the Prophet's absences from Medina while at war.

Apart from the resolution of conflicts and the general jurisdiction over provinces, none of the other functions which we can observe in the most minimal and rudimentary of states, such as the management of finances and the upkeep of law and order, are reported in the narratives which have come down to us, such as would lead us confidently to attribute a system of government to the Prophet.

8. We may note, in this connection, that most historians do not omit to give a list of the officials – governors, generals, judges and so on – appointed by each of the caliphs or rulers. Indeed, they show such deep interest in this issue as to have made it the object of specific studies, pursued with immense diligence and industry, thus exhibiting an acute consciousness of the scientific importance of such work. But when they turn to this aspect in the biography of the Prophet, they make vague and inconsistent statements, departing from the methods they normally follow in their inquiry into other periods. In our view there is no single historian who is an exception to this rule, apart from Rifa'a Al Tahtawi[13] who, as we shall mention later, in his *Nihāyat al-Ijāz fī Sīrat Sākin al-Ḥijāz*,* reproduces the earlier conclusions of the author of *Takhrīj ad-Dalālāt as-Sama'iyya*.**

9. The more we delve into the nature of the juridical and administrative systems at the time of the Prophet, the more obscure and vague it becomes. Our

---

* "Concise Biography of the Illustrious Resident of the Hijaz" [1982].
** "Deducing the Prophetic Sayings" by 'Ali ibn Muhammad Khuza'i [1985].
13 Rifa'a Rafi' at-Tahtawi, a relative of Muhammad al-Baqir Zain al-'Abidin. Died in 1873.

The System of Power at the Time of the Prophet

uncertainty drives us from one study to another and from one instance of confusion to another, until we are at a complete loss. We find ourselves faced with a still greater difficulty that seems to form the source and the heart of all the confusions and perplexities we have so far encountered. Certainly, it is the most important of the questions we have come across. Should our reasoning succeed in finding an acceptable solution to this quandary, then all of our other problems will lose their edge and our uncertainty and confusion will evaporate.

However, as we approach this question our steps grow hesitant and our pace uncertain. This is initially due to the extreme complexity of the problem and to the countless obstacles it holds in store for the student. Clearly, without the aid of God there is not the least hope of success in disentangling the rights and wrongs of this issue. Thus, the sheer audacity involved in tackling this inquiry is likely to cause an outcry among those who believe that religion is a fixed thing, closed to examination by reason or the effort of the intellect.

Despite these risks, we beseech the Almighty for His succour and guidance in this endeavour, by means of which we hope to dispel the obscurity which surrounds this issue and, God willing, arrive at the manifest and reassuring truth of it.

The question that we propose to treat here concerns the exact nature of the Prophet's mission. Was he or was he not at one and the same time a head of state and government as well as the Messenger, entrusted with propagation of the faith, and the spiritual leader of a community of believers?

5
Prophecy and Power

There is no objection to inquiring into whether or not the Prophet was a monarch – Prophecy and monarchy are two completely different phenomena – The thesis according to which the Prophet was also a monarch – The Prophet's system of government as depicted in detail by certain theologians – Analysis of what may be considered as the apparatus of state at the time of the Prophet – The jihad – Financial administration – The Prophet's exemplary behaviour – The putative appointments of governors by the Prophet for the administration of the land – Was the establishment of a temporal state one of the objectives of the Prophetic mission? – God's message and its implementation – On Ibn Khaldun's idea that Islam is a legislative system with the purpose of conveying and enforcing the message of the revelation – Objections to this thesis – The thesis according to which the Prophet's regime had all the characteristics of a government – Our possible ignorance of the system put in place by the Prophet – A discussion of this possibility – Realising the pristine simplicity of the system of authority established by the Prophet – The simplicity of the Muslim faith – Discussion of this idea

1. We need have no qualms about embarking on a study intended to ascertain whether or not the Prophet was a king. There is no reason to think of such an undertaking as a threat to religion, or to the faith of the scholar involved in it. A careful examination of this issue will show that such a study is not so harmful as to push the believer beyond the limits of his or her faith, or to shake the principles of a pious person and lead them astray.

Islam and the Foundations of Political Power

The question might well seem grave and daunting because it bears upon the stature of the Prophet and touches on the position occupied by him. However, notwithstanding this impression, to pose this question is in no way to question the foundations of the Islamic faith. This kind of enquiry is probably of recent origin among Muslims. Such questions were not addressed directly by any theologian in former times, and, as a result, no theologian has succeeded in forming a clear notion of these ideas. There is no reason, therefore, why theologians should regard a mere consideration of the question as to whether or not the Prophet was a Messenger as well as a king, an illicit innovation [*bida'a*]. Nor is it justified to see this as deviation or heresy. In fact, this enquiry does not fall under the category of religious dogmatics, normally a subject reserved for theologians. Rather, it falls into the realm of scientific research. Hence, it may be pursued all too safely.

2. We know that the mission of a prophet is very different from the position of a king and there is no necessary link between these two. The prophetic function confers a special stature on its incumbent amongst the people. The office of king is of a very different kind. In general, kings are not prophets or messengers of God. Likewise, how many among the messengers of God were kings? In fact, most prophets of whom we know were only messengers of God.

Jesus, son of Mary, was a Messenger sent to preach Christianity. This did not prevent him from advocating obedience to Caesar and endorsing his authority. It was He who pronounced these far-reaching words to his followers: "Render unto Caesar what is Caesar's and unto God what is God's".[1]*

The Prophet Joseph, son of Jacob, had been an official in the dominion of Rayyan ibn al Walid, the Egyptian Pharaoh. Afterwards, he served another potentate, Qabus ibn Mus'ab.[2]

We know very few figures in the history of the prophets with the combined attributes, decreed by God, of a prophet and a king. Was the Prophet Muhammad one of them, or was he just a prophet and not also a king?

3. To our knowledge, none of the theologians has a clear opinion on this matter. We are not aware that any of them ventured to deal with it. Nevertheless, if we

---

* The translation given here is from Mark 12.17.

1 Matthew 22.21.

2 *Abu al-Fida, History*, vol. 1. [*Tārikh Abi al-Fidā'* ["The History of Abu al-Fida"] was authored by Abu al-Fida [1273–1331] from 1315 to 1329. This historical treatise begins with pre-Islamic Arabia up to the author's present day. The work was extended by many scholars after al-Fida's death and was published in 1754 by the German scholar Johann Jakob Resike.]

were to proceed through simple inference, one could state that the lay Muslim is inclined to regard the Prophet as a Messenger-King sent by God. He or she would also accept that through Islam, the Prophet founded a state in the political and civil sense of the term, a state of which he himself was king and lord. This seems to be the prevailing view among Muslims and one that is implicit in the way they conduct their affairs. It is also perhaps the most widespread opinion among theologians. For, whenever they address themes related to this subject, they tend to favour the point of view according to which early Islam was a political entity and a state founded by the Prophet.

The argument advanced by Ibn Khaldun in The Muqaddimah is along the same lines, as it treats the caliphate as a vice-regency of the Lawgiver, having the function of protecting the faith and governing the land – thus investing it with the attributes and functions of kingship.³

4. Rifa'a al-Tahtawi* cites passages from *Takhrīj ad-Dalālāt as-Samaʿiyya* which present a frank elaboration of this position:

> He whose knowledge is limited, and whose vision is confined to external appearance, thinks that most of the activities of a government are recent inventions rather than reflecting models of old. He believes that someone who works within a temporal order of things does so outside the tradition laid down by the Prophet. Hence he has a poor view of these functions. It is with a view to restoring the truth about this subject that I have stated here all that I know about the diverse functions of government. This is in order to show, for each of them, their essence and the manner in which they manifest themselves. I have enumerated there the functions instituted by the Prophet and the names of the companions to whom he allotted them. The purpose of doing this is to enlighten those who are in charge of these functions today, so that they may turn in gratitude to the Almighty who has steered them to the very duties enshrined in the law of Islam, to the tasks which were entrusted to the Companions who had the qualifications to perform them, and which God has ordained for them in advance.⁴

---

* 1801–76.

3 Ibn Khaldun, *The Muqaddimah*. See in particular ch. 31, "On Dynasties, Royal Authority, Government Ranks".

4 Rifaʿa al-Ṭahṭawī, *Nihāyat al-Ijāz fī Sīrat Sākin al-Ḥijāz* ["The Ultimate Summary of the Life of an Inhabitant from the Hijaz", 1876].

Islam and the Foundations of Political Power

Rifa'a goes on to provide a brief survey of the various civil duties and procedures, such as the management of local administration, defence of the community and so on, which made up the Islamic system of government, together with the positions, professions and other associated dispensations. He thus reconstructs the model in force at the time of the Prophet, citing the functions associated with the Prophet and the general duties linked to the Great Imamate, the more important among the offices of the State, such as that of the minister, the *hajib* [government official], the secretary of the state, the supervision of the sacrificial rite of *Budn*,[5] the office in charge of the distribution of water,[6] as well as the functions of education and religious training, the teaching of the Qur'an, writing and *fiqh* [Muslim body of jurisprudence], the office of the *mufti* [Sunni legal scholar], the imam in charge of prayer and, lastly, the *muezzin* [the one who proclaims the call to prayer]. Referring next to the translators, secretaries and assistants of the army and the *diwan* [council of state], he asserts that the origin of administrative offices dates back to the Prophet. Next, he mentions political institutions, such as regional administration, the judiciary and the functions associated with it – the recording of testimonies, deeds, contracts, legacies and orders for expenditure – offices of estate agents and watchmen at buildings. Finally, he mentions the positions of market inspectors [*muhtasib*], town criers, watchmen, intelligence agents, prison guards and so on. He attributed such claims not only to a minority of biographers, but to all of them.

5. There is no doubt that the Prophet's authority included certain elements that could be compared with those of a temporal government, thereby reflecting some aspects of power and regality.

6. The first example that comes to mind during the time of the Prophet is that of the jihad [struggle]. We know that the Prophet took armed action against those of his people who opposed his religion: that he conquered their lands, confiscated their property and turned their men and women into prisoners. Nor is there any doubt that the Prophet had designs on certain regions beyond Arabia and that he was preparing to deploy his armies in different areas. In his lifetime he confronted the Byzantine state to the west and made overtures to the kings

---

5 A sacrifice of a cow or camel that was practised in Mecca at the time.
6 A service that was offered to pilgrims at the time.

of Persia (to the east), Ethiopia, Egypt[7] and so on, for conversion to the faith he was preaching.

It is evident from a glance that the jihad is neither carried out specifically to rally men to the new faith, nor to make them believe in God or His Prophet. Rather, the jihad is launched to reinforce an established power and to extend the empire.

Religious preaching is above all a call to God. It takes effect only by word, by the change wrought in the heart through persuasion, by an impact on human sensibility. Resort to force or coercion is not compatible with a mission meant to guide people to their salvation and to purification of their faith. No prophet, throughout history, has ever tried to bring people to believe in God by the sword, or conquered a people so as to convince them to join his faith. The Prophet himself underscored this principle through the words of the revelation:

> *There is no compulsion in religion.*
> *Right guidance has been distinguished from error.*[8]
> *Call to the way of your Lord with wisdom and fair counsel, and debate with them in the fairest manner.*[9]
> *So remind! For you are but a reminder,*
> *You are not their minder.*[10]
> *If they argue against you, say: "I have surrendered my face wholly to God, I and those who followed me." Say to those to whom the Book has been revealed and to those without a Book: "Have you surrendered?" If they surrender, they are guided aright. If they turn away, your duty is merely to announce the message. And God is Ever-Attentive to His creatures.*[11]
> *Will you then compel people to become believers?*[12]

These principles clearly show that the mission of Muhammad (like that of his predecessors) is to be fulfilled by means of persuasion and exhortation to the good and not by force or violence. Accordingly, if the Prophet took recourse

---

7   The allusion here is to the battle of Mu'ta and the expedition dispatched to Abni under the commandment of Usama ibn Ziyad.
8   Qur'an 2.256.
9   Qur'an 16.125.
10 Qur'an 88.21.
11 Qur'an 3.20.
12 Qur'an 10.99.

to force it was not in order to call people to the faith, or to transmit God's message to them. It can only be interpreted as a means to establishing a state and an Islamic government. We know that no government can survive without recourse to coercion and constraint. It is in this light that the belligerent acts of the Prophet should be understood.

7. We have said that the jihad was one of the features of the Islamic state and is one of the typical undertakings of any temporal state. We could add other examples in this connection.

At the time of the Prophet the administration of finance was an important exercise. This was due to the importance of revenue and the expenses incurred, as well as the numerous measures required for the collection of funds from different sources – the religious tax, the booty, the tithe paid by the People of the Book and the allocation of these funds to pay for diverse expenses. The Prophet allocated these procedures to tax collectors and agents. There is no doubt that financial administration is a major function of the state, indeed the most important office of any government. It is alien to the position of the Messenger and far removed from the typical behaviour of prophets.

8. Perhaps the best example is the one reported by Tabari, according to which the Prophet organised the administration of Yemen and allocated responsibility for the different geographical sectors to various men. Thus, he appointed 'Amr ibn Hazm as governor of Najran; Khalid ibn Sai'd ibn al-'As as governor between Najran, Rimah and Zubeid; Amir ibn Shahr in Hamadan; Ibn Badham in Sanaa; Tahar ibn Abi Hallah in 'Ak and al-Ashahrain; Abu Musa al Ashari in Ma'rib; and Ya'la ibn Abi Umayya in Janad. Also, Mu'ad ibn Jabal served as an itinerant teacher across the districts of Yemen, Hadhramaut, and so on.

One might provide other examples from the same period, displaying the characteristics of a state, a government and the emergence of a temporal power. Anyone considering the issue from this perspective might conclude that the Prophet was at once an envoy of God and a political or worldly ruler.

9. If these examples are taken seriously and the Prophet is considered to be both a Messenger and a temporal ruler, then we will be inevitably faced with another difficulty worthy of consideration. Were the constitution of the Islamic state, and the actions pursued in that regard, alien to the mission entrusted to the Prophet? Or were they part of the message revealed to him by God?

Prophecy and Power

To look upon the Prophet's domain as completely distinct from the preaching of Islam and alien to the Prophetic mission, represents a point of view which to my knowledge has no support in the creed of the Muslims. As far as I can recall, no Muslim treatise makes such an assertion. Nevertheless, this thesis could be urged without incurring blasphemy or heresy. In fact, it is not unlikely that some such consideration lies behind the outright rejection by certain Muslim sects of the idea that the institution of the caliphate is an inextricable component of Islam.

That the Prophet could engage in an activity so distinct from his prophetic mission need not perplex us any more than the circumstance of his dominion acquiring a temporal complexion intrinsically different from his religious mission. Although such a claim goes against the grain of our thinking, being rather alien to the discourse of Muslims, it does not deserve criticism or censure. Whether from the point of view of Islamic principles, the nature of the prophetic mission, or indeed the very spirit of the legislation and the tradition of the Prophet, nothing leads to rejecting such an opinion. We can even find substantial arguments in favour of this idea in those same sources, though we also recognise it as an exaggerated position.

10. The thesis that the state founded by the Prophet represents a fundamental entity, well integrated into the prophetic mission – indeed a fulfilment of it – appears to find general favour with Muslims. It is implicit in their habits of thought and action, and is corroborated in their principles and doctrines. It is clear that rational acceptability of this thesis requires us to show that the Prophet's obligation was to put his message into practice after he had conveyed it – that he was responsible both for the transmission and the implementation of his message.

11. It is noteworthy that the scholars who have investigated the significance of the Prophet's mission, and whose works we have had the opportunity to consider, have omitted to mention the implementation of religious principles as a constituent of the prophetic message. The one exception is Ibn Khaldun, who held that of all religions, Islam alone links the religious message with action designed to put it into practice. He elaborates this point of view in many passages in his historical work, Al Muqaddimah. He gives a detailed treatment of it in the chapter dealing with the offices of the Pope and Patriarch among Christians, and that of a Rabbi among Jews.[13]

---

13 Ibn Khaldun, *The Muqaddimah*, ch. 31, "On Dynasties, Royal Authority, Government Ranks", p. 183.

Islam and the Foundations of Political Power

From this passage, it is apparent that Ibn Khaldun considers Islam to be simultaneously a message, a system of legislation and the implementation of this legislation. Among all the religions, Islam is unique in encompassing both spiritual and temporal power.

12. In our opinion, this is an unfounded interpretation. It is not justified by any authoritative source. Worse still, it is in contradiction to the significance of the Prophet's message. As we have already seen, it is also incompatible with the prerequisites of purely religious dispensation. Moreover, were this interpretation sound, its proponents would have been confronted with another problem – the same problem we anticipated at the beginning of this work, and which has taken us to a wholly different line of inquiry.

If it is true that the Prophet instituted a political regime; or if he at least set into motion a process leading to such a state of affairs, why should this "state" have remained bereft of the paraphernalia typical of any temporal power? Why did scholars inquiring into this subject fail to identify the governors of this regime? Why was it not possible to know the procedures for the nomination of judges? Why did the Prophet not speak to his subjects about government and about the rules of popular consultation? Why did he keep the theologians in doubt about such an important subject as the system of government that he himself had introduced? These and a host of similar questions permeate our minds when we consider this topic. As a result, we are obliged to trace the origins of this confusion, uncertainty and inconclusiveness – however we might describe it – which seems to pervade the construction of the system of government during the time of the Prophet. How could this have happened and what hidden, motivating forces might have been at work?

Those who uncritically champion the view that Muhammad both preached a new faith and established a new state – maintaining that this "state" as founded by the Prophet was organised and administered by virtue of divine inspiration – find themselves compelled to also maintain that the regime of the Prophet reflected a degree of perfection inaccessible to human reason. When questioned regarding the apparent imperfection of the system of control of this "state" and the ambiguity of the procedures of governance, they will most likely defend themselves by recourse to one of the following arguments.

13. The author of *Takhrīj ad-Dalālāt as-Samā'iyya*¹⁴ proposes a relatively simple solution to this daunting problem; Rifā'a al Tahtawi follows suit. They presume that the government during the time of the Prophet was comprised of all the necessary components for a state: agents and services, organised systems, clearly defined rules and detailed procedures. So much so, that it was felt there was no need to revise or improve the system. However, there is no benefit in dwelling further on this point after all that we have already discussed in the preceding paragraphs on this very matter.

14. An adherent of the above-mentioned view might still argue that there is nothing to stop us from accepting that the apparatus of a state was already developed and firmly established at the time of the Prophet; that it comprised all the components of a perfect governmental system, befitting a regime led by an envoy of God, a man inspired by God and aided by His angels. If we lack knowledge of the details of this organisation, and of the exact, systematic fashion in which it was handled, it is only (so it might be argued) because chroniclers and historiographers failed to pass on the relevant information; or because, if they did so, it remains, for one or another reason, unknown to us: of knowledge you have been granted but little.¹⁵

15. A scientific mind will not dismiss this line of reasoning without examining it. On the contrary, we should have no qualms in admitting that we are probably ignorant of a lot of historical facts about the Prophet. Our ignorance is certainly far greater than our knowledge, not only with respect to this simple subject, but also regarding a good many other subjects. Scholars must always be prepared to admit that there are facts which elude their understanding; and that their duty lies, precisely, in striving relentlessly to discover everything still inaccessible to the mind and to draw ever newer conclusions. For this is how science survives and continues. Our possible ignorance of certain matters should not stop us from believing in the truth of the propositions conveyed to us [that which is known to us]; from considering these as genuine scientific truths on which we may rely as a basis for judgement, or from which we may determine a chain of sources, or even draw conclusions, until we find evidence to the contrary.

---

14 Ali ibn Muhammad Khuza'i, *Takhrīj ad-Dalālāt as-Samā'iyya* ["Deducing the Prophetic Sayings", 1985].
15 Qur'an 17.85.

For all these reasons we accept the possibility that our information about the system of rule by the Prophet might be incomplete and that one day we might well discover that it was indeed an exemplary system of government. Once again, as long as present evidence is not refuted by new data, this possibility need not prevent us from wondering about the real origin and significance of the confusion and ambiguity concerning the Prophet's system of authority which we have pointed out.

16. There is yet another way of resolving this issue. Most of what we understand today as the functions of a government, of the systems essential to any form of organised power, are in fact contingent conventions or artificial accretions by no means typical of a nascent, simple state. An authority that is close to nature has no place for conventions that are useless to the requirements of a simple human life.

When we consider this we see that whatever pertains to the state of the Prophet leads to a single observation: that it had none of the essential devices which political experts attribute to temporal governments. However, this has never been considered a defect. The absence of these devices has never been seen as a failing of the system set up at the time, or as a sign of anarchy or malfunction. This could be a plausible explanation for the apparent uncertainty that we can observe in the Prophet's state.

17. It is an established fact that the Prophet Muhammad liked simplicity and detested all forms of affectation. His entire life, private as well as public, reflects the greatest informality. He did not allow any disparities in the regulations he imposed over people's behaviour, whether public or private, or in the rules he laid down. His words and behaviour alike proclaim the ideal of simplicity, as can be seen in the remark he made to Jabir ibn Abdullah al-Balji: "Be concise in your speech," he urged him, "and when you have conveyed what you have on your mind, do not belabour it any more".[16]

He mixed with people without false reserve and his relations with them were all marked by a noble simplicity. Apparently, the Prophet loved to joke with his friends and would say to them: "There is no distinction between you and me. God dislikes those who discriminate between friends."[17] It is said that: "when the

---
16 Al Mubarrad, *Al-Kāmil* ["The Perfect One", c. 826–98].
17 Ali ibn Burnhan Din al-Halabi, *As-Sīra al-Ḥalabīya* [c. 1886].

Prophecy and Power

Messenger of God was in a situation where he had to choose between two things, he opted for the simpler alternative, as long as it did not entail committing a sin."[18] In his advice to Abu Musa al-Ashari and Mu'adh ibn Jabal, cited above, he urged them to behave gently rather than aggressively and with reassurance rather than intimidation.

Expressing his aversion to all forms of affectation and hypocrisy, the Prophet addressed this prayer to God during his last pilgrimage: "Lord, let our pilgrimage be an act of piety, free from vanity and pretence." And God on his part instructed him in these words:

Say: "I ask you no wage for it, nor am I one who dissembles."[19]

While conveying divine decrees, the Prophet would ask the people to follow the simplest rules and to avoid dissimilitude. Thus, he said: "Follow what is incumbent on you in any particular matter insofar as it lies within your power." And again: "This is a rigorous faith, but do implement it with gentleness." As the Qur'an explicitly says:

He chose you and did not burden you in religion ...[20]

When we look at the legislation introduced by the Prophet, we will be hard put to find a single dispensation which does not boil down to principles of the simplest sort. For example, the rules about prayer do not hinge on calculations about the position of the sun or the pathways of the stars. The timings of the prayers rests rather on perceptible events which anyone may check for themselves – for example, the observable trajectory of the sun in the sky. The signal for the start of the fasting period or the pilgrimage (or other such rites) is to be found in the phases of the moon, which are plain for everyone to see and do not require calculations or elaborate observation. The phases of the moon are open to sense perception and involve no special procedures or implements. Thus, the start of the fast is triggered by simple observation. The relevant hadiths address the subject in these terms: "We are an illiterate people ... Begin the fast as soon as you

---

18 Al-Bukhari, *Traditions islamiques* [c. 810]. [It will perhaps clarify the meaning of this hadith and its relation to the present context by translating it as: "When he had to choose between two things, he always opted for the simplest solution, except where it led him to commit a sin."]
19 Qur'an 38.86.
20 Qur'an 22.78.

notice the new moon."[21] There was no need, then, to count hours and minutes. Everything was anchored rather in sensory perception, uncomplicated by any sense of mystery. As the Qur'an says:

eat and drink until the white streak of dawn can be distinguished from the black streak. Then complete your fast until night-time.[22]

The Prophet, who was unlearned,* was a messenger to a people without learning. There were no disparities in his private or public behaviour, or in the rules he introduced.

It is to these features that we may attribute the essential character of the political system in place at the time of the Prophet. As we have seen, it was a system characterised by the greatest simplicity and conformity with the state of nature. In contrast, most existing systems of government prove to have developed innovations and conventions which we have come to take for granted as if they were essential traits, that is, an indispensable basis of political regimes. This is the case despite the fact that upon reflection it turns out to be anything but the case.

In sum, what would appear to be ambiguities, improvisations or intrinsic inefficiencies in the Prophet's political order are but proof of the simplicity and the unsullied purity of his nature.

18. If we had to choose between the two positions we have presented here, we would no doubt prefer the latter, for it is the closer of the two to the religious point of view. However, it does not seem right to hold such a position, for upon reflection one could well see that it is not in fact correct or well founded.

Certainly, in the numerous systems which are introduced by modern governments, the vast majority of the conventions and innovations which characterise them answer neither to the soundest principles of nature nor to the most authentic of instincts. Nevertheless, it is beyond doubt that the majority of the institutions that constitute systems of government of recent origin do not entail artifices of a redundant kind, nor are they arbitrarily called into being. They are

---

* Abdel Razek takes the word *ummi* in the sense given to it by mainstream Sunni traditions. He does not seem to be aware of more recent interpretations, which take it to refer rather to being non-Jewish – the Prophet from the Abrahamic line having no Jewish roots.

21 *Al-Fath al-Bārī fī Sharh Sahīh al-Bukhārī* ["Grant of the Creator"], 1428 is a Sunni commentary by Ibn Hajr Asqalani on *Sahīh al-Bukhārī*, one of the six major hadith collections.

22 Qur'an 2.187.

not in contravention of natural propensities. On the contrary, they are essential as well as useful. No government with the least claim to civility can afford to do without them.

For instance, we would scarcely see it as an expression of nature, or of a rudimentary form of organisation, if a government lacked a budget with which to exert control over revenue and expenditure, or if it lacked administrative offices designed to monitor internal and external affairs. Yet such expedients were wholly unknown at the time of the Prophet and are hardly mentioned by him.

Consequently, it would be wrong to seek to account for the omissions we might notice in the system of government headed by the Prophet in terms of an adherence to the most basic of principles and a rejection of superfluous conventions. Instead, we should explore other possible views in attempting to resolve this perplexity.

6
Islam: A Message from God rather than a System of Government; A Religion rather than a State

The Prophet was a messenger from God, not a king – The authority of a divine messenger contrasted with the authority of a temporal ruler – The specific excellence of the Prophet – Clarification of terms such as "emperor", "government" and so on – The Qur'an denies that the Prophet was a temporal ruler – Tradition follows suit – The character of Islam is antithetical to what appear to be the hallmarks of a state

1. We have seen that anyone inclined to think that the Prophet united in himself the functions of an envoy of God with those of a temporal ruler has to reckon with insurmountable obstacles. No sooner than one manages to get around a problem in this connection, one is faced by a new, equally daunting obstacle. Therefore, there remains only one alternative to consider in the hope of finding a clear and logical method capable of skirting all obstacles or insurmountable difficulties, and saving us from getting lost in mazes of guesswork or insuperable hurdles. This is to acknowledge that Muhammad was strictly a Messenger, entrusted with a purely religious mission, uncompromised by any desire for kingship or temporal power. This mission cannot in any way be interpreted as a campaign in quest of a kingdom in the general sense of this term. According to this view, Muhammad was no more and no less than an envoy sent by God, in no way different from his brethren-prophets who preceded him. He was not a king, nor the founder of an empire, nor someone preaching in favour of a kingdom.

This point of view is rather uncommon and perhaps unpalatable to Muslims.

It has the advantage, however, of being logical and having solid evidence in its favour.

2. Before we embark on an elucidation of this point of view, we must be on guard against the risk of an error if one is not perceptive and one is not cautious. The calling of the Prophet presupposes a certain degree of authority or power over his people. However, this is not the same as the power or authority that a temporal ruler wields over his subjects. Thus, one must remain on guard against confusing these two forms of authority or power. The difference between them is so great that it could be seen as an opposition. The authority which Moses and Jesus exercised over their followers had nothing in common with the authority belonging to a king. This remains true for the great majority of prophets.

3. A genuinely religious mission requires a certain perfection of its bearer. Beginning with his appearance: a freedom from physical or mental defects, or anything that might make him repulsive to others. Moreover, insofar as he must lead his people, he needs to possess a dignity calculated to command their respect, and likewise to endear him to the men and women who follow him. Lastly, he must enjoy a moral perfection born, first of all, of his character and, secondly, of what he inevitably acquires from his relationship with the Almighty. The bearer of a prophetic mission must, furthermore, command a social pre-eminence amongst his own people. This is indicated in the following hadith:

> *God never sends a messenger to a people other than somebody who is one of them – the noblest and least vulnerable of them.*[1]

Similarly, a prophet's mission calls for a forcefulness of character, capable of driving his message home and rallying the people around him. For God does not ordain affairs idly. If he elects to convey His word through a prophet, His will is to see the work accomplished. It is to ensure that it leaves an indelible stamp on the destiny of the universe and to carve the truth of existence on the bosom of humanity.

---

1 A hadith which is reported by the two great masters, Al-Bukhari and Muslim ibn al-Hajjaj [821–75], as part of a long prophetic tradition: "Thus prophets are selected among the noblest men within their people." See 'Abd ar-Raḥman ibn 'Ali ibn ad-Dayba, *Taysīr al-Wuṣūl ila Jāmi' al-Uṣūl min Ḥadīth ar-Rusūl* ["Facilitating Access to all the Roots of Law (al-Uṣūl) from the Prophetic Accounts", c. 1913].

A Message from God rather than a System of Government

"We sent no messenger except to be obeyed, by God's leave."[2] God does not in the least suffer the word of truth to be lost, or to be devoid of influence. Under no circumstances would He brook a setback or a humiliation to be visited upon His apostles (as the following verses of the Qur'an attest):

Messengers before you were mocked. But those who mocked them were overwhelmed by that which they used to mock.[3]

Say: "Travel the earth and see what was the destiny of liars."[4]

God wishes to vindicate the truth with His words, and utterly to uproot the unbelievers, in order to vindicate the truth and nullify falsehood, even if the wicked shall hate it.[5]

Our Word has already passed to Our servants the messengers, That they shall be granted victory, That Our troops shall prevail.[6]

We will assuredly come to the aid of Our messengers, and of those who believed in this present life, and on the Day when the witnesses rise up, a Day when the excuses of the wicked shall be worthless. A curse shall fall upon them and an Evil Abode awaits them.[7]

The status of a prophet necessitates the possession of a power greater than that which a temporal ruler wields over his subjects, or that a parent exerts over their children. He may have a similar role as that of a political head in the affairs of his community. However, this role involves a function which is unique to the prophet and which he does not share with anyone else. It is a function that enables him to see directly into the hearts of people, to rend asunder their veils so as to gain insight into their innermost recesses. The prophet must penetrate to his followers' deepest layers of sensibility, the mainsprings of their sentiments of love and hatred that lead them to commit acts of sin or of virtue. He must gain access to the hidden patterns of their mind, to its secret nooks and crannies, where their innermost fears and preoccupations, the springs of their motives and their character are to be found. Without doubt, the Prophet exercises this

---

2 Qur'an 4.64.
3 Qur'an 21.41.
4 Qur'an 6.11.
5 Qur'an 8.7–8.
6 Qur'an 37.171–3.
7 Qur'an 40.51–2.

function outwardly at the level of mass politics. But above all, he also exercises it at the level of the type of relations that exist between associates or partners in an alliance, a master and a servant, a parent and a child, or the intimate relations between a husband and wife that remain unknown to others. The Prophet has the outward as well as the inward aspects of things within his sight. He deals with relations of body as well as mind, on earth as well as in heaven. He is concerned with things of this world as well as the next.

We see, then, that the function of a prophet entails a gift, to an extent more than we could imagine, for communion with the hearts of men, and likewise, a capacity to mould them in their entirety. Besides, it is worth noting that the career of the Prophet Muhammad was distinguished by a number of features from that of his predecessors.

4. Muhammad was elected by God for a summons to humanity at large. By the will of God, he was able to convey his message in full. He nursed it until it was brought to completion and its virtues were carried to a state of perfection, free altogether from confusion or ambiguity. He ensured that the faith was dedicated in its entirety to God alone. Such success requires the greatest talent any human being can have. It requires the greatest willpower, of the sort conferred by God on the most righteous among his chosen apostles; and it requires a divine aid commensurate with the immensity and the universal scope of the mission. The terms in which the Almighty invokes the Prophet's mission are all too indicative in this regard:

> *The bounty of God upon you has been immeasurable.*[8]
> *... for you are in Our Very Eyes.*[9]

The following hadiths convey the same sense:

> "By God! God will never humiliate you."
> "In God's name, and without exalting myself [I vouch that] I am the noblest of the progeny of Adam."

It is for this reason, in light of the mission with which the Prophet was charged, that his ability was so wide-ranging. His command and authority were absolute.

---

[8] Qur'an 4.113.
[9] Qur'an 52.48.

A Message from God rather than a System of Government

Everything pertaining to government was part of his prerogative. Every form that the exercise of authority may take was implicit in his leadership of the community of believers. If, as reason suggests – and judging from the record of the apostles who came before Muhammad – the form of control by a prophet over the affairs of his people must vary with each instance, we can see that he had a claim, more than all the others, to the most extensive power over his followers and their complete obedience. The sheer potency of his message, the authority invested in him by a divine mission and the penetrating impact of his honest preaching led to its triumph over error, in accordance with God's will, and to its perpetual presence on earth. Such power is of heavenly provenance; it is conferred by God upon one who has been touched by an angel bearing a divine revelation. It belongs to the category of sacred power, attributable to prophets alone, containing nothing in the nature of imperial suzerainty;* no instance of temporal authority comes anywhere near it. It denotes the kind of sovereignty that is inherent in an authentic apostleship of God, charged with the delivery of a divine message and not the sovereignty of a ruler. It is a religious proclamation and prophetic authority in one, totally distinct from the power enjoyed by princes and potentates.

We must reiterate our warning against the danger of confusing the two types of power – one which the prophet holds in his capacity as an envoy of God, the other being characteristic of kings and princes.

The power that the prophet exercises over his people is of a spiritual nature. It is born of a faith cherished in the heart. Submission to such power is wholehearted and carries in its wake submission on the part of the body. By contrast, the power of a prince is material. It elicits a submission of the body in which there is no involvement of the heart. The former aims at a leadership over men in the path of justice and initiation into the Truth. The latter has to do with the organisation of the vital requirements of a society and the occupation of land. The former aims at the establishment of a religion; the latter serves strictly the interests of this world. The former provides religious and spiritual direction; the latter is a purely secular enterprise. How far they are from each other! What a distance lies between them – between religion, on the one hand, and politics, on the other!

5. There is another aspect of this question which deserves attention. There are terms that serve as synonyms in a certain context, while in another they carry

---

* The authority of a suzerain (a superior feudal lord).

different meanings. In our representation of things, there are times when this fact gives rise to confusion, differences and controversy. This is precisely the case with notions such as monarchy, kingdom, government or caliphate, or the king, potentate, leader, prince and so on.

When we ask whether or not the Prophet was a king, what we are in fact seeking to know is whether he had a quality or trait other than what belongs to an apostle of God, and hence whether he could in principle be said to have been concerned or not with setting up a political entity. In the sense that we employ the term "king" (and it is immaterial to us if another equivalent term, such as "caliph", "sultan" or "prince" were to be used instead), it quite simply means the holder of a power among people who constitute a political or civic unity. Similarly, we understand "government", "state" or "kingdom"* in the sense that political scientists generally attach to these terms.

We do not deny that Islam constitutes a religious union and that, as such, Muslims are one community. The Prophet advocated this sense of unity, and what is more, he achieved it quite effectively before his death. Of this religious union, he was the head, the unparalleled Imam, a leader inspired by the Almighty; hence an absolute sovereign whose commandments none could defy and whose decisions none was able to oppose. He secured this union by means of the word and by means of the sword. God granted him victory over his opponents. He accorded to him the assistance of His angels. He enabled him to succeed in his cause, which he had cherished, and to deliver the message entrusted by God. Consequently, he possessed a power that no king would ever have over his people either before or after him.

The Prophet is more caring of the believers than they are of themselves ...[10]

Who so disobeys God and His Prophet has strayed far in manifest error.[11]

If one wants to call this spiritual unity a "state", or to describe the absolute power wielded by the Prophet in terms of imperial or caliphal power, and so to characterise the Prophet as king, caliph or sultan, let them be at liberty to do so. They are entitled to use what after all are words and therefore do not trouble us. For what is most important (as we have already pointed out) is the sense one attaches

---

* These three terms are in English in the original Arabic text.
10   Qur'an 33.6.
11   Qur'an 33.36.

A Message from God rather than a System of Government

to these words, the sense that we have outlined above in the clearest possible fashion.

What is really essential to determine is whether the Prophet's sovereignty over his people stemmed from his role as the Apostle of God or whether it was an imperial phenomenon; whether the occasional display of power in his actions points to the presence of a state, or of a spiritual authority; and whether the nature of the entity over which he presided was political, or whether it was rather a strictly and exclusively religious community. In a word, again, what is essential to determine is whether the Prophet was only an apostle of God or both a "king" and a Messenger from God.

6 The text of the glorious Qur'an corroborates this thesis, maintaining that the Prophet had no interest whatsoever in political power. Its verses indicate that the Prophet's religious work and preaching remained scrupulously free from anything in the nature of temporal power. Thus:

> *Who so obeys the Messenger thereby obeys God. Who so turns away, We did not send you as their overseer.*[12]
>
> *Your people called it a lie, though it is the Truth. Say: "I am not your keeper; Every account has its closure. And you shall surely know."*[13]
>
> *Follow what has been revealed to you from your Lord – there is no god but He – and turn away from the idolaters. Had God willed, they would not have worshipped idols. But We did not appoint you their keeper, nor are you their guardian.*[14]
>
> *Had your Lord willed it, all on earth, every single one, would have believed. Will you then compel people to become believers? No soul can believe except by God's leave.*[15]
>
> *Say: "O mankind, the Truth has come to you from your Lord. Who so embraces guidance, embraces guidance for his own soul's good; Whoso goes astray, leads his own soul astray. Nor am I your guardian."*[16]

---

12 Qur'an 4.80.
13 Qur'an 6.66–7.
14 Qur'an 6.106–7.
15 Qur'an 10.99–100.
16 Qur'an 10.108.

Islam and the Foundations of Political Power

We sent you not as guardian over them.[17]

Have you observed him who took his own caprice as his god? Are you to act as his warden?[18]

We sent down on you the Book for mankind, in truth. Who so follows guidance does so for the good of his soul; who so strays in error does so to its detriment. You are not their guardian.[19]

If they turn away, it is not as their guardian that We sent you: yours is but to convey the message.[20]

We know best what they say, And you are not a tyrant ruling over them. So remind with the Qur'an whoever fears My threat.[21]

So remind! For you are but a reminder, You are not their minder. But he who turns away and blasphemes, Him God shall torment with the greatest of torments.[22]

We can see that the Qur'an explicitly forbids a view of the Prophet as a custodian of men, in charge of their affairs, possessing dominion over them, or for that matter a tyrant[23] given to coercion. Nor that he was allowed the use of force for inducting the people into the faith. A person who shuns any form of control or dominion over men can scarcely be regarded as a head in the temporal sense. For domination, power or authority – of unlimited scope – is definitive of a temporal position of power.

Muhammad is not father of any man among you, but he is the Prophet of God and the Seal of Prophets. God has knowledge of all things.[24]

---

17 Qur'an 17.54.
18 Qur'an 25.43.
19 Qur'an 39.41.
20 Qur'an 42.48.
21 Qur'an 50.45.
22 Qur'an 88.21–4.
23 It comes to me that I have read in a book that I can no longer trace back, that *al-Jabbar* is used as synonym for king by some Arabs, which clarifies the expression "Thou art not an *al-Jabbar* over them" [Qur'an 50.45, in some translations]. What I find in reference books is that kings are called *Jabra*, that it was common to say "*Al-Jabbar* has risen", referring to the Gemini constellation, since it looked like a king sitting on a throne. It was also commonly said "an al-Jabbar arm's length", to mean, probably, the king's arm's length.
24 Qur'an 33.40.

A Message from God rather than a System of Government

The Qur'an is equally clear that Muhammad did not have any claim over his people save those stemming from his proclamation of the prophetic message. Concomitantly, if he had been a worldly ruler, he would have had corresponding rights over his people. Temporal power entails rights, privileges and consequences quite distinct from those pertaining to a prophetic mission. This is highlighted in the following verses:

> Say: "I have no power to do myself good or harm save as God wills. Had I known the Unseen I would have done myself much good, and no harm would have touched me. I am merely a warner, and a herald of good tidings to a people who believe."[25]

> Are you perhaps about to set aside some of what is being revealed to you, and with which your heart feels constricted, because they say: "If only a treasure were sent down upon him or an angel would accompany him"? You are but a warner – and it is God Who is Guardian over all things.[26]

> You are but a warner, and for every people there is a guide.[27]

> Say: "I am but a human being like you, to whom inspiration is sent. Your God is in truth One God. Who so hopes to meet his Lord, let him perform deeds of righteousness, and associate none with the worship of his Lord."[28]

> Say: "O people, to you I am but a manifest warner."[29]

> "I am merely one who receives inspiration, merely a clear warner."[30]

> Say: "I am but a human being like you, to whom inspiration is sent. Your God is in truth One God."[31]

The Qur'an emphasises, then, that Muhammad was no more than a messenger, succeeding the many who came before him. It makes it equally plain that the Prophet's task was confined to relaying the divine message to humanity; that this task was to be pursued to the exclusion of everything else; and that he was not to enforce what he was called upon to convey, or to compel the people to abide by it. The following verses make this clear:

---

25 Qur'an 7.188.
26 Qur'an 11.12.
27 Qur'an 13.7.
28 Qur'an 18.110.
29 Qur'an 22.49.
30 Qur'an 38.70.
31 Qur'an 41.6.

If you turn away, know that Our Messenger is enjoined only to convey the manifest message.[32]

The Messenger is enjoined only to convey the message, and God knows what you reveal and what you conceal.[33]

Have they not reflected? There is no madness in their companion. He is merely the one who delivers a distinct warning.[34]

Was it so strange to people that We revealed to a man among them: "Warn mankind, but give glad tidings to those who believe that they have precedence in virtue with their Lord"?[35]

Whether We show you part of what We promised them or whether we cause you to die, it is your duty to convey the message, but Ours is the accounting.[36]

Are messengers enjoined to do anything other than deliver a manifest message?[37]

If they turn away, yours is only to convey a manifest message.[38]

We sent you only as a herald of glad tidings, and a warner.[39]

We made it easy upon your tongue, to give glad tidings to the pious, and to warn a people who harbour such malice.[40]

We did not bring down the Qur'an upon you to make you suffer; rather, it is a Remembrance to him who fears God.[41]

If they turn and go, upon him rests his burden, and upon you your own. If you obey Him, you will be guided aright.[42]

But you We sent only as a herald of glad tidings and a warner.[43]

I have only been commanded to worship the Lord of this city which God has sanctified. To Him all things belong. And I have been commanded to be a Muslim, and to recite the Qur'an.

---

32 Qur'an 5.92.
33 Qur'an 5.99.
34 Qur'an 7.184.
35 Qur'an 10.2.
36 Qur'an 13.40.
37 Qur'an 16.35.
38 Qur'an 16.82.
39 Qur'an 17.105.
40 Qur'an 19.97.
41 Qur'an 20.1–3.
42 Qur'an 24.54.
43 Qur'an 25.56.

A Message from God rather than a System of Government

Who so is guided, is guided merely for his own good. Who so strays into error, say: "I am merely a warner."[44]

"If you deny the truth, other nations before you also denied it. The Messenger is bound only to deliver the message with total clarity."[45]

O Prophet, We have sent you as a witness, a herald of glad tidings and a warner, one who calls to God, and a luminous lamp.[46]

We sent you not but to all of mankind – a herald of glad tidings and a warner. But most of mankind has no understanding.[47]

"and then reflect. There is no touch of madness in your fellow townsman. He is merely a warner to you that great suffering is imminent."[48]

You are but a warner. We sent you with the Truth, a herald of glad tidings and a warner, and there is no nation but a warner had passed it by.[49]

They said: "Our Lord knows that we are sent as messengers to you. Ours is only to convey a manifest declaration."[50]

Say: "I am but a warner, and there is no god but the One, All-Conquering God..."[51]

Say: "I am not a novelty among messengers. I know not what is to be done to me or you. I merely follow what is revealed to me. I am nothing but a manifest warner."[52]

We have sent you as a witness, a bearer of glad tidings and a warner..."[53]

Obey God and obey the Messenger and be on your guard. If you turn away, know that Our Messenger is enjoined only to convey the manifest message.[54]

For they had said to those who disliked what God had revealed: "We will obey you in certain matters only." And God knows full well their secret thoughts.[55]

---

44 Qur'an 27.91–2.
45 Qur'an 29.18.
46 Qur'an 33.45–6.
47 Qur'an 34.28
48 Qur'an 34.46.
49 Qur'an 35.23–4.
50 Qur'an 36.16–17.
51 Qur'an 38.65.
52 Qur'an 46.9.
53 Qur'an 48.8.
54 Qur'an 5.92.
55 Qur'an 47.26.

Islam and the Foundations of Political Power

Say: "I pray solely to my Lord, and associate none with Him."

Say: "I have no power to do you evil or bring you right guidance."

Say: "None can grant me shelter from God, nor will I ever find, apart from Him, any hideout. I merely convey a proclamation from God, and His messages."[56]

7. If we now pass from the Qur'an to the sunna, we shall find even more explicit statements and still clearer evidence to this end.

The author of the *As-Sīra an-Nabawīya*[57] mentions an incident where a man presented himself to the Prophet with a matter in hand. Finding himself in the presence of the Prophet, he was overawed and shook with fear. The Prophet said to him, "Be calm, for I am neither a king nor a tyrant. I am but the son of a Qurayshi woman who used to partake of salted meat." It is said in a hadith that being given a choice by the angel Israfil between the combined role of a prophet and a king, on the one hand, and a prophet and a slave, on the other hand, the Prophet turned to Gabriel for advice. Gabriel cast his eyes downwards, as if to suggest that humility was the better option. (In another version, Gabriel explicitly says so.) Therefore, Muhammad opted for the status of a prophet and a worshipper.

This is again a definite sign that the Prophet was not a king, that he did not seek to be one and that he did not even harbour such an ambition in the depths of his heart.

One looks in vain to either the Qur'an or the hadith for a simple allusion, whether explicit or implicit, which might give succour to the proponents of a political interpretation of the Islamic faith. These two sources are the ultimate, indisputable reference points in the Islamic faith. They are accessible to everyone. Anyone is free to look through them for an argument, or the semblance of an argument, in favour of this theory. It will be in vain. Unless we wish to content ourselves with suppositions, which in any case can never be a substitute for the truth.

8. Islam is a religious predication: a summons to God. It is a system that aspires to a reformation of the human condition; to redirect humanity to the path leading to God. It is a means to the attainment of everlasting beatitude,

---

56 Qur'an 72.20–3.
57 Ahmed Zayni Dahlan, d. 1886. *Iktifā' al-Qanū'* ["The Satisfaction of Frugality"], Edward Van Dyck: Cairo, 1896.

A Message from God rather than a System of Government

the reward, promised by God, to the most righteous among His subjects. It is a religious union, one that God has willed for all of humanity, encompassing all the lands on earth.

It is a holy and pure preaching which calls out to all humanity, regardless of the colour of their skin, to hold fast onto the rope of the One God; to become a single community, a single fellowship united in the worship of the One God. It is a call to the lofty ideal of a universal peace intended to elevate the world to a fitting state of perfection and bliss, to the mercy of the Lord in heaven and earth and to His good in both worlds.

This summons to humankind to come together as fellows in faith is in keeping with the principles of reason. It is to be found in the human potential for its realisation.

Furthermore, God assures us that this wish for the unification of humankind will be granted:

> *So do not imagine that God shall fail His promise to His messengers ...*[58]
>
> *God has promised those among you who believed and did righteous deeds to make them inherit the earth, as He caused those before them to inherit, and to establish their religion on firm foundations – the religion He sanctioned for them – and to instil peace of mind following their fear. And let them worship Me, and associate nothing with Me. Thereafter, who so disbelieves, these are the dissolute.*[59]
>
> *It is He Who sent His Messenger with Guidance and the religion of truth, that He may exalt it above all religions. Let God suffice as witness.*[60]
>
> *Who is more wicked than one who fabricates lies from God while being called to Islam? God guides not a people who are wicked.*
>
> *They mean to put out the light of God with their mouths, but God shall perfect His light, even though the unbelievers detest it. It is He Who sent His Messenger with Guidance and the religion of truth, to send it victorious over all other religions, even if the polytheists detest it.*[61]

It is conceivable that humanity may one day come to be unified within a single

---
58 Qur'an 14.47.
59 Qur'an 24.55.
60 Qur'an 48.28.
61 Qur'an 61.7–9.

religion and so form a single community. By contrast, the hope that the world may come under a single government, that it may form a single political order, would seem almost alien to human nature. As such, it is probably not intended by God.

Nevertheless, such a prospect does fall into the category of secular endeavours, having been set by divine grace as an objective for human reason. In this domain, individuals have been left free to pursue this endeavour in accordance with their own understanding, knowledge and interests, their passions and predilections. For, in His infinite wisdom God so wished that people should differ from one another:

> *Had your Lord willed, He would have created mankind a single nation. But they continue to differ, save for those to whom God has shown mercy. It is for this reason that He created them.*[62]

In order that the growth of civilisation on earth is brought to completion, and the design of God realised, God wished that there be competition among people:

> *Had God not restrained mankind, some by means of others, the earth would have become chaotic. But God is gracious towards His creation.*[63]

What this concerns is a principle of worldly life, where the Prophet refused to legislate or intervene, saying only, "You are better informed than I am in affairs of the temporal realm."

For it is indeed a principle of temporal life. Besides, we know that this whole sphere of life, with everything which it involves and is sought after, does not in the eyes of the Almighty call for any particular intervention on His part – nothing, that is, which falls outside the scope of God-given attributes of humanity: human reason, human sentiments, knowledge and desires. They do not feature, therefore, in the commitments and preoccupations of the apostles of God.

9. We ought not to be misled in this regard by the fact that we do find activities in the career of the Prophet which appear to be political and which seem to indicate an exercise of imperial or stately power. Nevertheless, upon closer

---

62 Qur'an 11.118–19.
63 Qur'an 2.251.

A Message from God rather than a System of Government

examination we comprehend that these activities were in fact nothing of the sort; rather, they were simply a set of means, among others, employed by the Prophet to reaffirm his teachings and reinforce the new faith.

It is not surprising that the jihad should be one of these means. It is without doubt a violent and brutal means, however, what do we know about it after all? Is not evil at times an unavoidable means to good? Is not destruction sometimes a necessary precursor for constructive accomplishment?

To those who say that coercion is undesirable we would say that it is a law of creation set down by God. The battle between truth and falsehood, between right and wrong, will continue till God accomplishes His design in the universe.

If God bestows His bounties on an arid land, if He makes it fertile and revives its verdure, making it blossom into fruit – would all this lose value if some obstacle had to be overcome in the process or a building demolished?[64]

> They said, "You have made war!
> By the Prophets of God, you were not sent
> Neither to kill nor to spill blood
> Ignorance, bad dreams and mistake is all this!
> You conquered by the sword after you conquered by the pen,
> When all noble men came to you spontaneously,
> The sword took care of the ignorant and the crowds
> Evil, if addressed by the Good, burdens you
> But when received by evil, dissipates.
> You taught them what they ignored
> Including war and its hideous face."[65]

10. The above discussion makes it clear that the Qur'an is not alone in ruling out the view that the Prophet, while pursuing his prophetic function, was at the same time calling for a state. Nor is the sunna alone in this respect. On the contrary, along with these sources, reason itself and everything which is implicit in the meaning and the nature of the prophetic mission points us away from this view.

The control that the Prophet exercised over the believers was strictly an exten-

---

64 Muhammad 'Abduh, *Risālat at-Tawḥīd* ["Treatise on the Unity of God", 1897]. [See Ishaq Musa'ad and Kenneth Cragg (trans.), *The Theology of Unity*, Kuala Lumpur: Islamic Book Trust, 2004.]
65 Extract from a poem by Ahmad Shawqi [1869–1932]. [In 1927 Shawqi was granted the title "Amir al- Sho'araa", "Prince of Poets". His anthology of poems *Al-Shawqīyyāt* [1890–1943] is seen as a major contribution to the Arabic literary tradition.]

sion of his prophetic function. It had none of the characteristics of temporal power. In all certainty, it was not a government; it was not a state; nor a political movement; neither was it the sovereignty of kings and princes.

We hope to have arrived at an answer to the afore-mentioned inquiry confirming the absence in the first Islamic community of any manifestations of a civil power or the preoccupations of a state. We hope to have shown that there was no governmental set-up, no offices of governors or judges and no establishment of administrative departments. In conclusion, we hope that the perplexity and confusion which we felt in the past have given way to clarity and peace of mind.

Book Three

The Caliphate and the Government throughout History

7
Religious Unity and the Arab People

Islam is not a religion exclusive to the Arabs – Arabness and religion – The simultaneous existence of religious unity and political diversity among Arabs – Islamic institutions have a religious rather than political character – The rudimentary nature of political differentiation during the time of the Prophet – The end of Prophetic authority with the death of the Prophet – The Prophet did not appoint a caliph to succeed him – The Shi'a doctrine of the succession of Ali ibn Abi Talib – The doctrine of the Jama'a (Sunni) in favour of the succession of Abu Bakr

1. As we know, Islam is a summons to a superior order which God has appointed for the whole world – for the east as well as the west, for Arabs and non-Arabs, for men and women, the rich and the poor, the literate and the illiterate. By means of this faith, God has willed the existence of a spiritual union that embraces all of humanity and gathers unto itself all the countries of this earth. Islam was never meant to be a uniquely Arab cause. It was not meant to form an Arab entity or an Arab religion. Hence, Islam does not recognise any claim to the superiority of a single nation over others, or of a language, or of a country or a generation, save the superiority conferred by piety. This is true even though the Prophet was an Arab, and so had a natural liking for Arabs, whom he acclaimed. And it holds true despite that the book revealed by God is in clear Arabic.

2. It was necessary that Islamic teaching should become manifest in this world, that it should prevail as an immutable truth among the truths of the universe,

Islam and the Foundations of Political Power

and that it should be transmitted to humankind, from the Lord, by a messenger chosen for this purpose. In His infinite wisdom and His unfathomable majesty, God willed that the man assigned to carry this message should be the offspring of Arabian tribes rather than some other race, from among the descendants of Ismail – more precisely, from the tribe of the Quraysh and the clan of Banu Hashim, namely, Muhammad ibn Abdullah.

The reason for this choice lies in the infinite wisdom of God, which we may or may not fathom:

> *It is your Lord Who creates what He wills, and it is He Who chooses – the choice is not theirs. May God be glorified and exalted far above what they associate with Him!*
>
> *Your Lord knows what their breasts conceal and what they openly declare.*[1]

Having been revealed in an Arabic book and through an Arab apostle, the new preaching naturally struck roots among the Arabs before spreading to other people. It was inevitable that the Arabs should be the first to hear the message, to be the bearers of the glad tidings and the warning, to receive the command to follow the path of the Lord, and to be among the first flocks whom the Prophet gathered onto the true path.

In this way, the Prophet divulged his message first to his close relatives and then to the Arabs, his people. Fortified by divine grace, he pursued his mission among them until they submitted totally to him. Under the guidance of the righteous Messenger, they became the first people to join together in the faith.

3. As is well known, the Arab lands were home to a number of peoples and tribes, differing from one another, speaking in different dialects and spread over a far-flung region. They also differed in their political organisation: some lived under the yoke of Byzantium, while others formed independent entities. As a result, there were huge differences in their systems of government, their methods of government, their customs and many aspects of their material and economic life.

These tribes, who had lived in mutual antagonism, came together under the banner of Islam. By the grace of God, they formed a great fellowship whose members were joined to one another by religious ties and by their common

---

1 Qur'an 28.68–9.

Religious Unity and the Arab People

acknowledgement of the authority of the Prophet who gathered them in the reach of his benevolence and mercy. Thus, they formed a single community [umma], obeying the authority of a single head consisting of the person of the Prophet.

This union of the Arabs, achieved during the time of the Prophet, was not – from whichever point of view one looks at it – a political union. It had none of the characteristics of a state or a government. It was nothing but a religious community devoid of any traces of politics. It was a union of faith, of religious doctrine, not a political union answering to the requirements of temporal power.

4. The life of the Prophet clearly illustrates the above. As far as we know the Prophet never intervened in the political affairs of the various tribes. He never sought to modify their system of government or to influence their administrative or judicial organisation. Neither did he try to intervene in the prevailing social or economic relations. There is no record of his having ever dismissed a governor, nominated a judge, set up a military guard or introduced measures to regulate the trade, agriculture or crafts of the people. He left all these matters to the people, openly declaring that they were better informed about them than he was himself. Each tribe was thus responsible for its particular conditions, its political set-up and the regulations, or (in case of an absence thereof) the anarchy under which they lived. What they were bound by was solely, as we have seen, the union brought about by Islam and the obligations which stemmed from it to honour its principles and its moral regulations.

It may be said that the principles and the moral rules and regulations advocated by the Prophet constitute a rather large number, governing as they do the elements of the majority of aspects of national life; encompassing such diverse areas or activities as a system of punishments, the organisation of an army, the conduct of jihad, transactions of trade, credit, mortgage; furthermore, including the principles of good conduct in a whole variety of situations, such as one's manner of sitting, walking, talking and so forth. One might well conclude that whoever it was that brought the Arabs together on the basis of such numerous rules designed to standardise their behaviour, their laws and their customs to the level required by Islam would in the process have unified their common way of life, and so necessarily created a unified state. The Prophet, then, would have to be viewed as the inspiration for and a ruler over just such a state.

However, a thorough examination of this notion illustrates that the whole set of legislation introduced by Islam, which the Prophet instructed the Muslims to follow, does not in the least resemble the sort of regulations enforced by a political authority or put in place in a temporal state. Moreover, these regulations taken in their totality do not make up even a limited part of the regulations and the legislative apparatus required by any temporal state.

In reality every principle of faith, every regulation that was introduced by the religion of Islam, including the rules of public morality and their accompanying set of sanctions, belongs to a purely religious sphere of legislation dedicated to God and to the search for salvation in the hereafter. Whether or not this religious goal is obvious, and whether it is effective in the sphere of worldly life, are not considerations that play an important role in the development of a religious legislation, or the mind of a Messenger.

The Arabs, even after being united under the law of Islam, maintained the diversity which we have already noted in their political sphere and in other areas of their civic life, social as well as economic. That is to say, that they constituted diverse, separate nations insofar as the conditions of those times permitted the realisation of such things as nations and governments.

This was the situation of the Arabs at the death of the Prophet: a religious union overseeing a diversity of nations, differing almost completely from one another. This is an established, indisputable fact.

5. One may suspect that this diversity that we have observed to exist during the time of the Prophet has remained unnoticed; that the impression of homogeneity with which historians have sought to depict this time has misled us. We most appreciate, to start with, that history is full of mistakes. How many a time has history been in error! How often has it led people astray!

In addition, we must remember that the diversities and animosities that were prevalent among the Arabs were to a large extent mitigated by the bonds of affection by which they were bound to Islam. This was a consequence of having been brought together under the banner of a common faith and having been led to adopt common customs and institutions.

A third factor to be taken into account is the result, mentioned earlier, of the spiritual leadership of the Prophet. It is not surprising to note that the differences among the Arab people were mitigated and their outward signs made to disappear, that the violence of the people was moderated and its intensity diminished. As the Qur'an declares:

Religious Unity and the Arab People

Remember God's bounties upon you, when you were enemies to one another, and how He brought harmony to your hearts so that, by His blessing, you became brothers. You had once been on the edge of a precipice of fire, and He saved you from it.[2]

Nevertheless, the Arabs continued to exist as different communities and formed separate political units. This situation was only natural. Its extent may have diminished, but it was in no way abolished.

No sooner had the Prophet died than the springs of difference and divergence among Arabs were powerfully reactivated. Every community rediscovered a sense of its separate identity and independent existence. The union realised at the time of the Prophet was now on the verge of dissolution. "The majority of the Arabs lapsed into apostasy at this time save for the inhabitants of Medina, Mecca and Taif."[3]

6. As we have seen, the unity of the Arab state was none other than the unity of the Islamic faith. It was not a political union. The leadership of the Prophet was of a spiritual and religious character rather than a temporal one. The submission to him by the Arab peoples was an act of faith. It stemmed from a religious conviction, not a political allegiance or recognition of the kind of authority typical of a government. The Arabs gathered themselves around him as an act of love for God, an act that earned them the favour of the divine revelation, the opening of the heavens and the commandments and prescriptions of the Lord. As the Qur'an says:

God did the believers a favour when He sent among them a Messenger, of their number, reciting to them His verses, purifying them and teaching them the Book and the Wisdom ...[4]

This, then, was the kind of role of leadership occupied by Muhammad ibn 'Abd Allah ibn 'Abd al-Muttalib al-Hashemi al-Qurayshi. It was not a status attained by him in his own right, nor on account of his parentage. It owed itself solely to his being an apostle of God.

---

2 Qur'an 3.103.
3 Abu al-Fida, *Tārīkh Abi al-Fidā'* ["The History of Abu al-Fida"], vol. 1.
4 Qur'an 3.164.

Islam and the Foundations of Political Power

Your companion has not veered from the truth, nor is he misguided. Nor is he giving voice to his fancies.[5]

The Prophet conversed with God via His angels. As he was the "Seal of Prophets",[6] none could exercise the religious role he had discharged after his death. None could inherit his mission; no one could succeed him. The mission of the apostle of God was not something that could be passed on. It was not something that could be bequeathed or delegated.

7. Thus, the Prophet died without appointing a successor – or someone who might discharge the function he had performed in the community. In other words, he did not make a single allusion in his whole life to the prospect of an Islamic or Arab state.

We can be certain – God preserve us from believing to the contrary – that the Prophet did not depart from the world without having delivered the entire message of God and having expounded to his community the entire set of principles of the new religion in a manner calculated to prevent any confusion or ambiguity. If the establishment of a state had indeed been part of his appointed purpose, how could he have left it so vague that the Muslims, finding themselves completely in the dark [after his death], fell to killing one another? Why did he not address the problem of succession or the head of state when holders of power always and everywhere regard it as a duty to settle this question as a matter of priority? How could he have left his people in such utter confusion as that which swept over them and instantly plunged them into the most vicious violence even before they could see his body to the grave?

8. We know that the Shi'a are unanimous in holding that the Prophet designated 'Ali ibn Abi Talib to succeed him as the Caliph of the Muslims. We will not discuss this doctrine here as it has little historical authenticity.*

According to Ibn Khaldun, "the texts that [the Shi'a] cite and interpret in line with their doctrines are as unknown to the masters of the Sunna as to the

---

* The author is expressing here, in crude terms, a view which is shared by traditional Sunni clerics as part of their polemics against their Shi'a colleagues. The strategy here, as is often the case, is outright dismissal of all narratives other than one's own, thus avoiding any real examination of the narrative. This is clearly shown by the passage Abdel Razek quotes from Ibn Khaldun in the following paragraph.

5 Qur'an 53.2–3.
6 Qur'an 33.40.

transmitters of the law. The bulk of the texts may well be forged or have been unreliably transmitted, or susceptible to a different interpretation from that to be found in their misguided approach to the matter."

9. The Zahiri Imam ibn Hazm aligned himself to a school of thought which had little following, to the effect that the Prophet expressly appointed Abu Bakr as the leader of the Muslim community after his death. This was supported [in his view] by the fact that the majority of the Muhajirun and the Ansar called Abu Bakr the Caliph of the Prophet, a term implying an act of designation by a predecessor and not simply a succession without prior indication – a usage which, we might add, is not accepted by everyone as linguistically correct. He advances an extremely long argument in favour of this view.

The above opinion seems to us extravagant and unjustified. We have consulted available works of philology and found nothing in them in support of Ibn Hazm's thesis. On the contrary, we observe the commonly agreed account of the differences over the nomination of Abu Bakr that broke out among his companions, together with the abstention of several important men among them. We also have the address of Umar-al-Khatab reiterating his remark on the day of the Prophet's death:

> O brothers, yesterday I told you something which was nothing more than a mere personal opinion. It was not from the Book of God, nor was it something that the Prophet confided in me. It was simply that I had assumed the Prophet would reign over us until the last person among us was dead. God has now left among us His holy Book, by means of which He guided His apostle onto the right path. If you hold fast to the prescriptions of the Book, you will be led along the same path. God has gathered you around the best among you, he who is the friend of the Prophet, his companion in the cave. Give your allegiance to him![7]

This statement, to which we could add others, proves that the thesis according to which the Prophet made provisions for his succession has no basis. It is an

---

7 When the Prophet died, Umar ibn al-Khattab rose among the people and declared: "Some hypocrites pretend that the Messenger of God has died, although, by God, the Messenger has not died! But he has gone to God, as Moses did once and stayed away from his people for forty nights before returning, when it was said that he had died. By God, the Messenger will come back and will cut the hands and feet of those who pretend that he died." Quoted by Tabari [Persian historian Muhammad ibn Jarir al-Tabari, 838–923. His most well-known work is *Tafsir al-Tabari*, 897, a commentary on the Qur'an].

indisputable fact that he gave no indication as to the form the government of Muslims ought to take after his death. He did not propose any rules in this regard to which the Muslims could refer.*

He did not return to the Eternal except when the faith had achieved perfection and its merits had been realised. The teachings of Islam shaped the truth of the world once and for all. It was then that the Prophet breathed his last. It was then that his mission was accomplished. It was then that the link between heaven and earth that he represented was severed forever.

---

* This is again a statement of the Sunni school of interpretation.

8
The Arab State

Authority after the time of the Prophet is necessarily political – The influence of Islam on Arabs – The birth of the Arab state – Differences among the Arabs on the question of allegiance

1. We have emphasised that the authority of the Prophet had a spiritual basis. It stemmed solely from his function as the Messenger. This function was completed with his death. With the demise of the Prophet, the type of authority that he had hereto exercised came to an end. Therefore, as there was no one who could succeed him in that position, no one was entitled to inherit his prophetic function.

If it became essential to institute leadership among the followers of the Prophet after his death, this had to be a new type of leadership, bearing no relation to the type of authority the Prophet had exercised.

It is only reasonable, and as one might expect, as well as in line with evidence, that there could be no religious authority after the Prophet. It is equally understandable that an authority of a new type, sharing nothing with the function of transmitting the divine message, and having no foundation in religion, should appear after him. This would have to be a secular power. Being secular, this was bound to be no more and no less than a temporal or political rather than a religious power. This is in fact what happened.

2. The Islamic teachings improved the lot of the Arab peoples on a number of levels. As soon as the Apostle of Islam called out to the people, they became a

Islam and the Foundations of Political Power

united nation, among the best during their time. Like every other nation, they prepared to conquer and to colonise.

A pure creed, unsullied by polytheism, a faith established solidly in the deepest part of the soul, a morality which the Prophet had raised to the highest peak, an intellect in accordance with the soundest nature, a sense of vitality accruing from the natural environment, a union under God capable of reconciling extremes and eradicating differences, binding them into a true fraternity under God – such was the condition of the Arabs at the death of the Prophet.

A people who had been reborn (for such were the Arabs at that point in time), could not suffer to return to their previous way of life after the Prophet, that is, to the unenlightened [*jahiliyya*] state of a primitive people, of tribes at war with one another, of political enfeeblement. When God provides the conditions to make a people strong and dominant, then this is exactly what the people become. They can do no other than to play their full part, undiminished, in the world. It was thus necessary that the Arab state come into existence, like others that had done so before it and others that would do so after it.

3. The Arabs were aware that God had granted them the essential conditions for the foundation of a state and that preliminary steps towards this end had been taken. Perhaps the Arabs had already sensed this before the death of the Prophet. Certainly, it was at this time that they began to confer with one another about the formation of a state in the political sense – something that had become feasible on the basis of the religious entity that was the legacy of the Prophet.

> Every prophet's work is followed by a monarchy which is built on compulsion.[1]

Thus, they conferred together at this time about building a state, creating a government as an act of original creation. This is why we now find in their discourse terms such as "prince", "principality", "minister", "ministry" and so on. They spoke of the army, the armaments, the higher ranks, group strength, the ability of self-defence, the power of coercion and the capacity to rescue. Such discussions were, no doubt, to do with nothing but temporal power and the installation of a state. As a result, as it is well known, rivalries began between the

---

[1] This means that every prophecy brings as a consequence the emergence of kings who prevail themselves of its legitimacy. See *Asās al-Balāgha* [c. 1100, a classical Arabic dictionary by al-Zamakhshari].

Muhajirun and the Ansar and between the companions of the Prophet. These rivalries persisted until allegiance was finally given to Abu Bakr. Hence, the latter became the first ruler in the history of Islam.

Upon examining the manner in which allegiance came to be paid to Abu Bakr, we can see that this allegiance had very much to do with a temporal or political pledge; that it had all the attributes of a newly created state; and that it was put into effect in the way that governments are established – that is, on the basis of force and coercion.

The new state created by the Arabs was an Arab state and an Arab power. While Islam, as we know, is a religion addressed to all humanity, a religion that is neither Arab nor non-Arab.

The Arab state was in fact founded on the basis of a religious predication. No doubt, this state provided for the preservation and direction of this preaching. Moreover, this newly founded state most likely had a major impact on the course taken by this religion. Certainly, the Arab state had a major impact on the evolution and the transformation of Islam from this time onwards. The fact remains, nonetheless, that it was an Arab state, promoting the power of the Arabs, serving their interests, enabling them to subjugate other countries on earth, which they colonised and exploited in the fullest sense of these words. They were no different in this regard from other powers that are able to conquer and colonise.

4. When the early Muslims assembled to choose someone to preside over their affairs, they already had a grasp of their new situation. The Ansar proposed to the Muhajirun an alternating arrangement of power. "Let us choose a prince from among yourselves", they said. "Then we shall choose one from among ourselves." Abu Bakr replied to them: "The princes must be nominated from amongst ourselves. Your party will provide ministers."

This is clear also from what Abu Sufian said at that time: "By God, I see a storm rising that can be settled only in blood. O Abd Manaf clan members, why is Abu Bakr involved in our affairs? Where are the two incapables, 'Ali and al-'Abbas?" After reciting he is said to have addressed 'Ali ibn Abi Talib, saying: "Open thy hands, so that I give you my allegiance." When 'Ali declined the offer, he recited verses by al-Mutalmiss:

> Accept the humiliation inflicted upon them only two
> Camels and pegs

The former remains bound in degradation,
The latter is broken and no one feels regret for it!

It is also clear from the fact that Sa'd ibn 'Ubadah* refused to give allegiance to Abu Bakr, saying: "By God, I would rather shower you with my arrows to the last one, soak my spear in your blood and hit you with my sword with all my strength. I would fight you together with my clan and all those who follow me from my people. I will not renounce by the truth of God. Even if the demons and all the men allied themselves to support you, I will not join them, and will wait until I know the judgement of the Almighty." After which he stopped praying with the community, participating in assemblies and, when in pilgrimage, practicing the rituals along with fellow Muslims. He stayed in this state of mind until Abu Bakr died.[2]

Muslims were aware, by that time, that they were building a temporal government. This is why they allowed themselves to disagree over accepting or rejecting such a government, since they understood it to be a matter of temporal (worldly) interest, not religious creeds. They considered that their divergences did not threaten their faith.

Neither Abu Bakr nor any other notable of the time pretended that leadership over Muslims was a religious office, implying that its rejection could amount to a rejection of the faith. To the contrary, Abu Bakr said: "O people, I am one of you. I do not know whether you will expect from me things that the Messenger of God could offer. God in fact has elected Muhammad over all his creation, and has protected him from error, while I am merely a follower, not a founder?"

However, numerous facts combined afterwards to confer to the position of Abu Bakr a religious character, which led some to imagine that he held a religious office by which he substituted for the Prophet. Thus, was born the allegation following which the office of ruler over Muslims was a religion function and a fulfilment of the Prophet's role.

One of the reasons for the emergence of such an allegation was the title of caliph (deputy) of the Prophet, which was given to Abu Bakr.

---

* A leader of the Ansar, the Medinan citizens who helped the Prophet Muhammad and the Muhajirun on their arrival to the city. He died around 630.

2 Mentioned by Tabari.

9
The Nature of the Caliphate

The advent of the title, the Caliph of the Prophet – The real meaning of the succession to the Prophet assumed by Abu Bakr – The reason for the choice of this title – How those who opposed Abu Bakr came to be regarded as apostates – Not all the opponents were apostates – On those who refused to pay the zakat – The ensuing battles were political rather than religious – The existence of real apostates – Abu Bakr's religious qualities – The propagation of belief in the religious character of the function of the caliph – The spread of this belief by kings and temporal rulers – Religion does not entail the institution of the caliphate

1. We have not yet established with certainty who devised the title of caliph for Abu Bakr. Nevertheless, we have noted that Abu Bakr agreed to be addressed as such, hence one could surmise that this implies his approval of the title of caliph for himself. We know that he placed this title at the head of the correspondence that he addressed via intermediaries to commanders of the Bedouin tribes that had turned apostate. These letters probably constitute Abu Bakr's first writings and thus the first documented instance we might have of the use of this title.*

2. The Prophet was doubtlessly the leader of the Arabs who brought about their unification, as we have already discussed. It would seem correct, in the light of Arabic linguistic usage, to attribute to Abu Bakr the expression the caliph (successor) of the Prophet or simply, in short, the caliph when he became the

---
* Mentioned by Tabari.

ruler of the Arabs, uniting them in the political sense as we understand it today. To do so is only to affirm the meaning of the idea of succession. It is simply to say that he came to his position after the Prophet, without imputing any further significance to this fact.

3. It is all too understandable that at a time of grave peril, when there was a resurgence of tempestuous passions within a people who had just come out of a state of witlessness, and who had not yet shed the tribal spirit of solidarity and the rude complexion and violent ways of Bedouin life – that in such circumstances Abu Bakr, seeking to found a new state and to re-unify scattered elements of the society, should have assumed a title with such splendid and alluring resonance and such a powerful appeal so as to succeed in his task. There are those who developed an argument from this, concluding that Abu Bakr's succession of the Prophet was a succession in the full sense of the word; that, because he had succeeded the Prophet, and because the Prophet was a vicegerent of God, Abu Bakr, too, had become the vicegerent of God. They would not have been wrong in their reasoning had the idea of succession meant what some people at the time took it to mean, but what no one today takes it to mean. For Abu Bakr himself, denying this interpretation, said: "I am in no way the vicegerent of God, only that of the Prophet."[1]

4. The title of caliph led a number of Arabs and Muslims to show to Abu Bakr a religious reverence similar to that which they had [shown] towards the Prophet. It led them to regard the function of the temporal head that he had discharged in the same manner in which they had regarded everything to do with their faith. For this reason, the insurrection against Abu Bakr was seen by these individuals as a repudiation of the faith – in other words, a form of apostasy. It is likely, in our opinion, that the interpretation that consigns those who opposed the power of Abu Bakr to the rank of apostates, along with the very expression "the wars of apostasy", has its source in this fact.

5. In fact, it is very likely that those who rose against Abu Bakr were not all apostates in the sense of repudiators of belief in God and His Prophet. They must have retained their Islamic faith while refusing for some reason to become part of the political apparatus headed by Abu Bakr, with neither resentment

---

[1] Ibn Khaldun, *The Muqaddimah*, p. 180

The Nature of the Caliphate

at their religious faith nor a vacillation over it or a weakening of it. They were certainly not apostates and the war that was waged against them ought not to have been waged in the name of religion. If it became necessary to fight them, this was for political reasons alone – reasons such as a defence of Arab unity and the Arab state.

We know that among those who refused to recognise the authority of Abu Bakr, and who were certainly not regarded as apostates, were certain men like Ali ibn Abi Talib and Sa'd ibn Ubadah.

6. Similarly, it is likely that among those against whom Abu Bakr waged war for their refusal to pay the zakat there were those who had meant through this gesture neither to reject the religion nor to commit apostasy. All they intended to do was refuse to submit to Abu Bakr's regime, just as some of the most eminent figures in the Muslim community (mentioned above) had done. It was but natural that having refused to recognise Abu Bakr as the temporal sovereign, having rejected his authority along with that of his government, they should refuse to pay zakat to him.

When we try to reconstruct the facts concerning those who rose against Abu Bakr from the mass of historical accounts that we have inherited on this subject, the mystifications and iniquities of historical writing come home to us all the more powerfully. Those who opposed Abu Bakr have collectively been treated as apostates, just as the wars against them have been called wars of apostasy. Nevertheless, a ray of light shines through this mist of mystification and future scholars may well follow the lead of this beacon and come to a proper understanding of the facts.

In this connection we can examine again the words of Malik ibn Nuwayra to Khalid ibn al-Walid. Malik was one of the so-called "apostates" who was executed upon the orders of Khalid (and whose skull was subsequently used as a prop for a cooking-pot over a camp fire). Malik declared to him, with manifest sincerity, that he continued to adhere to Islam, but that he was not prepared to pay zakat to Khalid's master (that is, Abu Bakr).

Thus, the dispute between the two men did not concern religion. It was a dispute between Malik, a Muslim who remained loyal to his faith, but who belonged to the tribe of Tamim* and Abu Bakr, a member of the tribe of Quraysh and the founder, moreover, of an Arab state whose leaders were all Qurayshites.

---

* One of the largest Arab tribes and a sister clan of the Quraysh. Also known as Banu Tamim.

Islam and the Foundations of Political Power

It was thus a dispute over the allocation of power. It was not over the principles of religion or the fundamental elements of faith.

Moreover, Malik's self-avowed commitment to Islam is not all that there is to it. 'Umar ibn al-Khattab confirmed the fact when he complained to Abu Bakr: "Khalid has murdered a Muslim. You must therefore put him to death." Indeed, Abu Bakr, too, bore witness to Malik's adherence to Islam when he replied: "I shall not kill him. For he has interpreted the order wrongly."[2]

Let us take another example, namely, of one of the poets alleged to be an apostate:[3]*

> We obeyed the Prophet when he was among us.
> O servants of God, what have we to do with Abu Bakr?
> Will we become a legacy [for someone else] when he dies?
> By God, its weight will break our backs.

We can see that these remarks indicate nothing but a revolt against Abu Bakr – a denunciation of his power and a refusal to give allegiance to him. At the same time, they express faith in the Prophet. They do not in any way detract from the principles of the Islamic faith.

Does not the history of this period inform us of 'Umar's reproach to Abu Bakr for having declared war on alleged apostates? Thus, he said: "How can you fight these men in these circumstances when the Prophet said, 'I have received the order to fight the people until such time as they realise that there is no god but God. The lives and properties of these will be protected, unless the law dictates otherwise. This judgement will rest with God.'"**

This is just a small glimpse of truth in the information which reached us, of truths that were nearly buried and were forgotten. Research can help find more.

7. We should not hesitate for a moment, therefore, to conclude that in the majority of cases the so-called wars of apostasy were against the regime of Abu Bakr and bore no religious significance. The conflicts that were involved were purely political. The people have since conflated them with wars fought in defence of the faith, whereas in fact they were quite devoid of a religious element.

---

* Mentioned by Abu al-Fida in his *History*.
** Mentioned by al-Bukhari.

2 Abu al-Fida, *Tārīkh Abī al-Fidā'* ["The History of Abu al-Fida", 1315–29].
3 Al-Khalil ibn Aws, brother of A-Hacin ibn Aws. See al-Tabari's *History*.

The Nature of the Caliphate

This is not the place for us to inquire into the real causes of the numerous battles that were fought against "apostasy". We cannot pretend to be in a position, were we tempted to undertake such an inquiry, to carry it through. Nevertheless, if we paid the utmost attention to the ancestry and the tribal affiliation of those who revolted against Abu Bakr, then some of the motivations which were at play during the wars of apostasy would become apparent. We would best understand these motives if we were to examine the relationships of the apostates with the tribe of Quraysh to which the holders of power in question belonged. We would need, further, to bear in mind the laws that operate in a nation which is yet in its infancy: the spirit of collective solidarity which serves as the road to power, as well as the mores and characteristics of the Arab people. If one had the opportunity to pursue this inquiry in the correct manner, all of these elements would have to be closely considered.

8. We readily admit that there were Muslims who did indeed turn to apostasy after the death of the Prophet. This was an occurrence that stemmed almost from the laws and the system of nature itself. We also admit, all too readily, the appearance of false prophets, as much during the lifetime of the Prophet as after his death. Experience shows us that pretence to prophecy is an all too real temptation for a charlatan capable of seducing the masses and misleading friends and admirers. People at large are only too liable to be taken in by a misguided charlatan who is skilled at luring people into error and leading them down the path of sin. This is why we accept that there was a group of people who renounced Islam, at the beginning of Abu Bakr's reign, for no other reason than that the Prophet was dead. It is for the same reason that various false prophets must have appeared among the Arab tribes at around this time.

The first act of Abu Bakr, then, was to wage war against the genuine apostates and false prophets until they had been defeated and their falsehood destroyed.

Abu Bakr initiated his move against the apostates in the newly constituted state by declaring war against them. It was then that the word "apostate" came into use. It was a justifiable term at the outset, referring to the true apostates. However, it subsequently came to be extended to all the Arab opponents, whether they were religious dissenters or political opponents who retained their Islamic faith. For this reason the wars waged by Abu Bakr have taken on a religious colour *in toto*. They have been described under the insignia of Islam and depicted as having been prosecuted under the banner of the faith. To have rallied around Abu Bakr was regarded as having rallied around Islam, while to have rebelled against his authority was seen as an act of apostasy and a sign of iniquity.

9. Another factor that might have helped to sow the seeds of confusion in the people, causing them to attach a religious dimension to Abu Bakr's reign in particular, was the personality of al-Siddiq.[4] Abu Bakr had enjoyed a place of honour with the Prophet, was the object of respectful mention in sermons and had acquired a prominent status among Muslims. Besides, he was given to emulating the demeanour of the Prophet and following his example in private behaviour as well as public deeds. He put all his energies into pursuing his role in the way of the faith and in applying, as far as possible, the procedures of the Prophet. It is therefore understandable that the place he occupied in the new state, of which he was the first ruler, should have been decked in the vestments of religion.

10. Thus, we can see that the title of caliph (the successor and vicegerent of the Prophet), together with the circumstances in which it was employed – circumstances which we have described only in part – were among the sources of the misconception, propagated among the ranks of Muslims, that the caliphate was a religious function. This led the people (wrongly) to ascribe the rank of the Prophet himself to whomever it was who held power over Muslims.

Thus, did the erroneous view gain ground, from the early days of Islam, that the caliphate was a religious office and that the caliph was the author, by delegation, of religious law.

11. It was in the interest of the rulers to propagate this fiction among the people. They did so with a view to protecting their throne and suppressing their opponents in the name of religion. They were relentless in inculcating this belief among the masses through numerous means* – the belief, namely, that obedience to rulers is tantamount to obedience to God; and rebellion against them, a rebellion against God. However, they were not contented even with this. They could not acknowledge what Abu Bakr had acknowledged, nor did they share his aversion. They turned the ruler into a representative of God on earth, His

---

* Exactly how numerous is something that historians might well have demonstrated had they been more willing to examine the facts.

4 The name by which Abu Bakr was known.

shadow, extending over His creatures: There is no God but He, glory to Him, far about their polytheism!"⁵

Thereafter the institution of the "caliphate" was included in the religious sciences. It was given the same status as the articles of faith. It was studied by Muslims in the same breath as the attributes of God and inculcated in the same manner as the profession of the faith, that is: "There is no other god beside God, and Muhammad is His messenger".

Such is the crime committed by despots and such are the consequences of their rule. In the name of religion they have misled the Muslims, veiled the roads to truth from their eyes and blocked the light of knowledge. In the name of religion they have usurped ownership over the Muslims. They have demeaned them and forbidden them to reflect on questions to do with politics. They have fooled them in the name of religion and set up obstacles, of all sorts, to intellectual activity. They have done all this to the point of depriving them of any frame of reference outside religion, even in purely political affairs, and in matters to do strictly with government.

These despots have likewise thwarted an understanding of religion and imprisoned Muslims within the mental boundaries set by them. They have prohibited all scientific thought liable to encroach on the domain reserved for the caliphate.

The sum effect of all this has been to kill the vital impulses of intellectual inquiry among Muslims. The impulse towards political reflection and investigation of caliphs as well as the institution of the caliphate has been effectively paralysed.

12. In truth, this institution which Muslims generally know as the caliphate has nothing to do with religion. It has no more to do with it than the lust for power and the exercise of intimidation that has been associated with this institution. The caliphate is not among the tenets of the faith – no more so than the judiciary or some other governmental function or state position. These exist by dint of nothing else but political fiat, with which religion has nothing to do whatsoever, which it wants neither to know nor to ignore; which it neither advocates nor repudiates. It is a matter which religion has left to humankind, for people to organise in accordance with the principles of reason, the experience of nations and the rules of politics.

What holds true in this case applies equally to the setting up of Islamic armies, the construction of towns and fortifications, the organisation of government

---

5 Qur'an 9.31.

– all matters which are of no interest to religion, but pertain rather to reason and experience, to rules of engagement in battle, to the art of building and the opinions of experts.

There is not a single principle of the faith that forbids Muslims to co-operate with other nations in the total enterprise of the social and political sciences. There is no principle that prevents them from dismantling this obsolete system, a system which has demeaned and subjugated them, crushing them in its iron grip. Nothing stops them from building their state and their system of government on the basis of past constructions of human reason, of systems whose sturdiness has stood the test of time, which the experience of nations has shown to be effective.

Praise be to God, who guided us onto the right path, and whose guidance was indispensable to the progress of this work. And greetings be on Muhammad, His Prophet, his companions, and all those who followed his path.

List of Sources referred to by Abdel Razek

Abd al-Salam ibn Ibrahim al-Laqani, *Itḥāf al-Murīd bi-Sharḥ Jawharat at-Tawḥīd* [The Disciple's Contribution to Commentary on the Essence of Divine Unity", 1831].

Abu al-Fida, *Tārīkh al-Mukhtaṣar fī Akhbār al-Bashar* [1315–29]. See Peter M. Holt (trans.), *The Memoirs of a Syrian Prince: Abu al-Fida, Sultan of Hamah*, Wiesbaden: Franz Steiner, 1983.

Abu al-Fida, *Al-Yawāqīt wal-ḍarb fī Tārīkh Ḥalab* ["The Gems and Afflictions of Aleppo's History", c. 1329], eds Muhammad Kamal and Falah al-Bakur, Aleppo: Dar al-Qalam al-'Arabi, 1989.

al-Asqalani Ibn Hajar, *Al-Fatḥ al-Bārī fī Sharḥ Saḥīḥ al-Bukhārī* [1428]. See Abdal Hakim Murad (trans.), *Selections from Fath Al-Bari*, Cambridge: Muslim Academic Trust, 2000.

al-Bajuri, *Sharḥ Jawharāt at-Tawḥīd* ["Explaining the Essence of Divine Unity", c. 1276], Cairo: al-Maktab al-Azhariyah lil-Turath, 2002.

al-Baydawi, *Ṭawāli' al-Anwār min Maṭāli' al-Anẓār* ["Manifestations from the Perspectives of the Horizon", c. 1300], ed. Abbas Sulaiman, Beirut: Dar al Jeel, 1991.

al-Bukhari, *Kashf al-Asrār 'an Uṣūl Fakhr al-Islām al-Bazdawī* ["The Unveiling of Secrets, Exposing the Origins Fakhr al-Islam al-Bazdawi", c. 800], ed. Muhammad al-Mu'tasim bi-Allah Baghdadi, 4 vols, Beirut: Dar al-Kitab al-'Arabi, 1994.

al-Bukhari, *Les traditions islamiques* [c. 810], trans. Octave Houdas and William Marçais, 4 vols, Paris: Ernest Leroux, 1903–14.

al-Bukhari, *Ṣaḥīḥ al-Bukhārī* ["The Authentic Hadiths of al-Bukhari", c. 810], ed. Muhammad Muhsin Khan, 9 vols, Alexandria: Al Saadawi Publications, 1996.

al-Eiji, Abdurrahman, *Al-Mawāqif fī-'ilm al-Kalām* ["Doctrines of Theology (al-Kalam)", 1355], Beirut: 'Alam al-Kutub, 1998.

al-Farazdaq, *Dīwān al-Farazdaq* ["The Anthology of Farazdaq", c. 720], ed. Karam al-Bustani, Lebanon: Dar Sader, 1990.

al-Farazdaq, *Naqā'iḍ bayna al-Jarīr wal-Farazdaq* ["The Polemic Poem between al-Jarir and Farazadaq", c. 720], Abu Dhabi: Isdarat al-Majma al-Thaqafi, 1994.

al-Halabi, 'Ali Ibn Ibrahim Nur-ad-Din, *As-Sīra al-Ḥalabīya an-Nabawīya* ["A Biography of the Prophet, c. 1460–1549], ed. Muhammad Ibn-Tawit al-Tungi, Damascus: Dar al-Ma'rifa, 1989.

al-Isfahani, Abu al-Faraj, *Kitāb al-Aghānī* ["The Book of Songs", c. 897–967], 25 vols, Beirut: Dar Sader Publishers, 2004.

al-Isfahani, al-Raghib, *Al-Mufradāt fi Gharīb al-Qur'ān* ["Rare Terms in the Qur'an", c. 1109], ed. Muhammad Khalil al-'Itany, Beirut: Dar al Ma'rifa, 1998.

al-Katibi, *Ar-Risāla ash-Shamsīya fil-Qawā'id al-Manṭaqīya* ["The Dazzling Work on the Foundations of Logic", c. 1276], ed. Mahdi Fadl Allah, Beirut: Al-Markaz al-Thaqafi, 1998.

al-Muti'i, Muhammad Bakhit, *Al-Qawl al-Mufīd 'ala ar-Risāla al-Musāma'a Wasīlat al-'Abid fi 'Ilm at-Tawḥīd* ["Useful Remarks on the Work entitled 'Means of Devotion in the Science of Divine Unity'"], Cairo: al-Matba' al-Khairiyya, 1908.

al-Muti'i, Muhammad Bakhit, *Haqīqat al-Islām wa Uṣūl al-Ḥukm* ["The Truth about Islam and the Foundations of Political Power", 1926], Cairo: Al-Matba'a, al-Salafiyya wa Maktabatuha, 1950

al-Mubarrad, *Al-Kāmil* ["The Perfect One", c. 826–98], ed. Muhammad Dali, Beirut: 1986.

al-Shawkani, *Irshād al-Fuḥūl ila Taḥqīq al-Ḥaqq min 'Ilm al-'Uṣūl* ["The Master's Guidance in Achieving Truth from the Roots of Law (science of al-Uṣūl)", c. 1759–1834], ed. Sha'ban Muhammad Ismail, Cairo: Dar al-Kutubi, 1992.

as-Suyuti, Jalal ad-Din, *The History of the Khalifas Who Took the Right Way* [c. 1400], trans. Abdassamad Clarke, London: Ta-Ha Publishers, 2008.

al-Tabari, *Tarīkh al-Ṭabarī* [c. 915]. See various translators and editors, *The History of al-Tabari*, 40 vols, New York: State University of New York Press, c. 1987–2007.

al-Taftazani, *Al-Fawā'id al-Bahīya fi Tarājim al-Ḥanafīya* ["The Splendid Benefits of Hanafi Biographies", c. 1357], ed. Abd al-Rahman 'Umera, Beirut, 'Alam al-Kutub, 1989.

al-Taftazani, *Maqāṣid at-Ṭālibīn fi Ilm Uṣūl ad-Dīn* ["The Aims of Students and the Foundations of Faith", 1383], ed. 'Abderrahman 'Amira, 5 vols, Beirut: Salih Musa Sharaf, 'alam al-kutub, 1989.

Sources

al-Ṭahṭawī, Rifa'a Rafi', *Nihāyat al-Ijāz fī Sīrat Sākin al-Ḥijāz* ["The Ultimate Summary of the Life of an Inhabitant from the Hijaz", 1876], eds Abderrahman Hasan Mahmoud and Farouq Hamid Badr, Lebanon: Fadak Books, 1982.

al-Zamakhshari, *Al-Kashāf al-Tanzil* [*"The Revealer"*, c. 1132], eds 'Ali ibn Muhammad al-Sayyid al-Sharif Jurjani, Ahmad ibn Muhammad ibn al-Munayyir and al-Hamawi Muhibb al-Din Muhammad ibn Abi Bakr, 4 vols, Cairo: al-Babi al-Halabi, 1972.

al-Zamakhshari, *Asās al-Balāgha* ["The Origin of Eloquence", c. 1100], 2 vols, Beirut: Maktabat Lubnan, 1996.

Arnold, Thomas, *The Caliphate* [1924], Oxford: Oxford University Press, Academic Monograph Reprints, 1998.

Baidaba, *Kalila and Dimna* [n.d.], trans. Ramsay Wood, London: Saqi Books, 2008.

Dahlan, Ahmed Zayni, *As-Sīra an-Nabawīya wal-Athār al-Muḥammadīya* ["A Biography of the Prophet and Muhammadan Traditions", c. 1886], Beirut: Dar al-Ma'rifa, 1960.

Ibn 'Abd al-Barr (Yusuf ibn Abdallah), *Al-Istī'āb fī Ma'rifat al-Aṣḥāb* ["The Comprehensive Book of Knowledge about the Companions", 1901], 4 vols, Beirut: Dar al-Kutub al-'Ilmiyya, 1995.

Ibn 'Abd Rabbuh, *Al-'Iqd al-Farīd* [c. 860–940]. See Issa J. Boullata (trans.), *The Unique Necklace*, 2 vols, Reading: Garnet, 2006–9.

Ibn ad-Dayba', 'Abd ar-Raḥman ibn Ali, *Taysīr al-Wuṣūl ila Jāmi' al-Uṣūl min Hadīth ar-Rusūl* ["Facilitating Access to all the Roots of Law (al-Uṣūl) from the Prophetic Accounts", c. 1913], Cairo: 'Issa al Babi al Halabi, 1978

Ibn Hazm, *Al-Faṣl fīl-Milal wal-Niḥal* ["The Book of Sects and Creeds", c. 994–1064], ed. Ahmad Shams al-Din, 3 vols, Beirut: Dar al-Kutub al-'Ilmiyah, 2007.

Ibn Khaldun, *The Muqaddimah: An Introduction to History* [1377], trans. Franz Rosenthal, 2 vols, Chichester: Princeton University Press, 1967.

Khuza'i, Ali ibn Muhammad, *Takhrīj ad-Dalālāt as-Sama'iyya* ["Deducing the Prophetic Sayings"], ed. Ehsan Abbas, Beirut: Dar al-Gharb al-Islami, 1985.

Muhammad 'Abduh ibn Hasan, *Risālat at-Tawḥīd* ["Treatise on the Unity of God", 1897]. See Ishaq Musa'ad and Kenneth Cragg (trans.), *The Theology of Unity*, Kuala Lumpur: Islamic Book Trust, 2004.

Qutb al-Dīn al-Rāzī, *Ar-Risāla ash-Shamsīya fīl-Qawā'id al-Manṭaqīya* ["The Dazzling Work on the Foundations of Logic"] with glossary by Qāḍī 'Abd al-Hakīm al-Siālakūtī, published by Sheikh Faraj Allah Zakī al-Kurdī, 1905.

Rida, Muhammad Rashid, *Al-Khilāfa wal-Imāma al-'Uẓma* ["The Caliphate and the Great Imamate"], Cairo: Manar Press, 1924. Also see Simon Wood, *Christian Criticisms, Islamic Proofs: Rashid Rida's Modernist Defence of Islam*, Oxford: Oneworld, 2007; and Henri Laoust, *Le Califat dans la doctrine de Rashid Rida* ["The Caliphate in the Doctrine of Rashid Rida"], Paris: Maisonneuve, 1986.

Rogers, Arthur Kenyon, *A Student's History of Philosophy* [1901], Oakland, CA: University of California Libraries, 2011 [digitised and reprinted].

Shawqi, Ahmad, *Al-Shawqīyyāt* ["The Anthology of Ahmad Shawqi", 1890–1943], Beirut: Dar al-Kitab al-'Arabi, 1992.

Van Dyck, Edward, *Iktifā' al-Qanū' bi-mā Huwa Maṭbū'* ["The Satisfaction of Frugality according to what is Written", 1896], Cairo: Alam al-Kutub, 1988.

Appendix
Notes on Authors referred to by Abdel Razek

Al-Baydawi, 'Abdallah ibn 'Umar, 1210–c. 1292

Muslim scholar and author of several theological treatises, including his major work, a Sunni commentary on the Qur'an entitled *Anwār at-Tanzīl wa Asrār at-Tāʾwīl* ("The Lights of Revelation and the Secrets of Interpretation"). This work is a summary of the Mu'tazilite commentary *Al-Kashāf* by al-Zamkhshari. It was edited by Heinrich Lebrecht Fleischer (Leipzig, 1846–8) and has not been translated into English in its entirety, but partial translations have been undertaken by Margoliouth (1894), Bishop and Kaddal (1957) and Beeston (1963). This work has proven popular in regions of the non-Arab Muslim world. However, al-Baydawi has been criticised for the occasional inaccuracy of his writings.

Abu al-Fida (Abu Al-fida' Isma'il Ibn 'ali ibn Mahmud al-Malik al-Mu'ayyad 'imad Ad-din), 1273–1331

Arab historian, geographer and sultan, born in Damascus. His works include *Tārīkh al-Mukhtaṣar fi Akhbār al-Bashar* ("The Concise History of Humanity", 1315–29). This takes the form of annals extending from the creation of the world to the year 1329. His *Taqwīm al-Buldān* ("A Sketch of the Countries", 1316–21) is founded on the works of his predecessors; ultimately Ptolemy. Parts of the work were translated and published in Europe as early as 1650.

Al-Isfahani, al-Raghib (Al-Cusayn ibn Muhammad ibn al-Mufaddal), c. 1050–1109

Islamic scholar and linguist who made contributions to tafsir, ethics and theology. His fame rests on his *Al-Mufradāt fi Gharīb al-Qur'ān* (c. 1109), a study of the semantics of the Qur'an, which had great influence on later scholars such as al-Faruzabadi (d. 1415) and Murtada al-Zabidi (d. 1791). Despite its influence and popularity, al-Isfahani's *Mufradāt* has been largely neglected by contemporary scholars of the Qur'an.

Islam and the Foundations of Political Power

Al-Muti'i, Muhammad Bakhit, c. 1860–1930

Mufti of Egypt from 1914 until 1921, born in Asyut. He served as provincial judge in various resorts, as *qadi* of Alexandria and of Cairo, and in a number of other high positions prior to his appointment as *mufti* of Egypt in 1914. He was a member of al-Rabita al-Sharkiyya ("The Oriental League"), but resigned in 1925 in protest at the efforts of some of its members to bring about the annulment of the intended trial of Ali Abdel Razek. In his work *Haqīqat al-Islām wa Uṣūl al-Ḥukm* ["The Truth about Islam and the Foundations of Political Power"] 1926, Bakhit criticised Abdel Razek's major essay *Islām wa Uṣūl al-Ḥukm*. Bakhit's work reflects his intellectual involvement with issues of his time, such as the status of women, conflict over the translation of the Qur'an and Islam's interaction with Western science and technology.

Al-Taftazani, Masʻud ibn ʻAmr ibn ʻAbdallah (Saʻad al-Din Masud ibn Umar ibn Abd Allah al-Taftazani), 1322–90

Renowned scholar and author on grammar, rhetoric, theology, logic, law and Qur'anic exegesis, born in Taftazan. Al-Taftazani's fame rests mainly on his commentaries, which came to be widely used in teaching at *madrasas* (Muslim institutions of learning and study) until modern times. He wrote a commentary of the Qur'an in Persian and translated a volume by the poet Sai'di from Persian into Turkish.

Al-Zamakhshari (Mahmud ibn Umar al-Zamakhshari), 1075–1144

Known as Djar Allah, al-Zamakhshari was a scholar who made important contributions to grammar, philology and lexicography. His most important grammatical work is the *Kitāb al-Mufaṣal fil-Naḥw* (ed. J. P. Broch, Christiania: Universitas Regiae Fredericianae, 1859, rev. 1879), a compendium on Arabic grammar that had considerable influence on Western grammars of Arabic. He is also known for his commentary on the Qur'an entitled *al-Kashāf*.

Ibn Khaldun (Abu Zayd Abdurrahman bin Muhammad bin Khaldun Al-Hadrami), 1332–1406

Arab historian and philosopher born in Tunis. He is the author of *The Muqaddimah* ("Introduction", 1377), also known as *Prolegomena*, a history of North

Appendix

African politics in which Ibn Khaldun analysed the rise and fall of dynasties and argued that group solidarity was vital to success in power. Ibn Khaldun built a career as a political operator, but in 1375, disillusioned, he withdrew into the Sahara desert, where he wrote *The Muqaddimah* in four years. Later he worked as a judge in Egypt. Over the past three centuries, Ibn Khaldun has been rediscovered as a prescient political scientist, philosopher and sociologist.

Rashid Rida (Muhammad Rashid ibn Ali Rida), 1865–1935

Major figure in the modern Sunni reform movement, follower of Muhammad Abduh and founder of the journal *Al-Manar*, which is devoted to the interpretation of the sources of Muslim belief and practice.

Index

Note: numbers in *italics* refer to appendix entries

'Abbasids, 29, 30, 50, 55
'Abd-al-Malik ibn-Marwan, 29, 30, 50
Abdel Razek, Ali, *1–17*
'Abduh, Muhammad, 4, 5, 11, 95n
Abu Bakr, 27, 36, 43, 45, 53, 105, 111
    allegiance to, 109–10
    war against apostasy, 112–16
Abu Bakr ibn al-Kamil, 50
Abu Da'ud, 60, 62
Abu Firas, 31n
Abu Musa al-Ash'ari, 60, 62, 72
Abu Sufian, 109
Abu Zayd, Nasr Hamid, 13, 14
Aden, 62
administration, 70, 72, 79, 101; *see also* governors
Al-Afghani, Jamal ad-Din, 4
Ahwaz, 55
Aleppo, 55
'Ali ibn Abi Talib (Ali), 45, 47, 60–1, 63, 104, 109, 113
    allegiance, 46–7, 109–10
alms-tax (*zakat*), 62, 63, 72, 113
angels, 60, 86, 92, 104
Ansar, 105, 109, 110n
Anushivan, 48
apostasy, 103, 112–13, 114–16
apostles, 83, 84, 85, 94
Aquinas, Thomas, 16
Arab Christians, 4

Arabia, 51–2, 70
Arabs, 30, 99–101, 115
    after Prophet's death, 103
    conflict against Abu Bakr, 112–13
    under Prophet, 102–3
    unification, 107–9, 111
Aristotle, 46, 48
army, 48, 70, 101, 108
Arnold, Sir Thomas, 38
As-Sīra an-Nabawīya, 62, 92
Al-Assamm, 52
Assyrians, 46
Atatürk, Mustapha Kamal, 2, 7
Ayyubids, 55
Al-Azhar University, 6, 8

Baghdad, 55
Bahrain, 55
Baidaba, 46
Al-Balji, Jabir ibn Abdullah, 76
Banu Hashim clan, 100
Banu Yafran (Ifren), 30
Batiniyya, 45
Al-Baydawi, 'Abdallah ibn 'Umar, 26, 60, *123*
Bedouin tribes, 12, 111
Bible, 40
blasphemy, 73
Budn, 70
Al-Bukhari, 61, 62, 77n, 82n, 114n

Index

Buyids, 55
Byzantium, 70, 100

Caesar, 40–1, 68
caliphate, 1–2, 5, 21, 54
   abrogation of, 2, 7, 9
   advent of title of, 111
   allegiance and, 46–7
   ambition leading to violence, 49–50
   arguments in support of, 35–6
   choice of term, 26–7
   duties and authority of, 27–30, 35
   in Egypt, 55–6
   misconceptions, 116–17
   monarchy and, 29–30, 69
   Muslim usage of term, 25–6
   Prophet's deputyship, 26, 27–8, 40
   Qur'an on the, 36–8, 39, 52
   reliance on coercion by, 47–8, 49
   religious law and, 28–9
   restoration of, 5, 6, 7, 9–10
   status of, 35–40
   subordinates of, 28
   succession, 104–6, 109–10, 111–12
   Sunni Muslims conceptions of, 10
   theory of power derived from God, 31–3
   theory of power derived from *umma*, 33–4
   uprisings and opposition to, 45–6, 47
Charfi, Abdelmajid, 15
Christianity, 68, 73
colonialism, 2, 108, 109
conquest, 61, 70, 71, 95, 108, 109
consensus, 29, 35, 38, 43–4, 51, 52
critical–historical approach, 15
critical reasoning, 5, 11

Dahlan, Ahmed Zayni, 62
despotism, 6, 7, 14, 41, 117
divine right of kings, 34
diwan, 70

East Africa, 7
Egypt, 2–4, 6–7, 12, 55–6, 71
Egyptian University, 8
Al-Eiji, Abdurrahman, 38, 43
Ethiopia, 71
European colonialism, 2, 4
European philosophy, 9, 16, 34

Faisal ibn Husayn ibn 'Ali, 51–2
Al-Farazdaq, 31
Fars, 55
fasting, 77–8
Fatimids, 55
Fazlur Rahman, 15
Al-Fida, Abu, 68n, 114n, *123*
financial administration, 72, 79
fiqh, 70
First World War, 51–2
Fouad, King of Egypt, 6, 9
France, 52
freedom of thought, 7, 13, 48
fundamentalism, 7–8, 13

Gabriel, archangel, 60, 92
Al-Ghassani, 63
government officials, 70
government systems, 53, 54, 70, 76, 78–9, 118
governors, 28, 64, 72
Great Britain, 2, 52
Greek science and philosophy, 44–5, 46

hadiths, 27, 38, 39, 40, 77, 82, 84, 92

127

Al-Hajjaj ibn Yusuf al-Thaqafi, 50n
Al Hallabi, 'Ali ibn Burnhan din, 61
Al Harith ibn 'Amr, 62
heresy, 73
Hicham ibn Abd al-Malik, 31
Hijaz, 7
Hobbes, Thomas, 9, 34
humanities, 5, 9, 14
Al-Hurra, battle of, 50n
Husayn, son of Fatima, 50
Husayn ibn 'Ali, prince of Arabia, 51
Hussein, Taha, 13
Al-Huyay'a, 33

Ibn Abbas, 50, 62
Ibn 'Abd Al Barr, Abu 'Amr, 61, 63
Ibn abi Hallah, Tahar, 72
Ibn 'Affan, 'Uthman, 60
Ibn al-Hajjaj, 82n
Ibn al-Zubayr, Abdullah, 50n
Ibn Anas, Malik, 44n
Ibn Aws, al-Khalil, 114n
Ibn Badham, 72
Ibn-Hanbal, 44n
Ibn Hazm, 39, 72, 105
Ibn Khaldun, 9, 16, 17, 26, 29, 35, 48, 52, 55, 69, 73–4, 104–5, *124–5*
Ibn Maymun (Maimonids), 63
Ibn Nuwayra, Malik, 113–14
Ibn Saman, 55
Ibn Shahr, Amir, 72
Ibn Tabataba, 55
Ibn Tulun, Ahmad, 55
Ibn 'Uqbah, 50n
Ibn Ziyad, Usama, 71n
ijmā, 29, 35, 38, 43–4, 51, 52
imam/imamate, 21, 25–8, 35–41, 44n, 46, 51, 56, 70
India, 7

Iraq, 52
Isfahan, 55
Al-Isfahani, al-Raghib, 25n, 32n, *123*
Islam, 54, 73–4, 86, 96, 101, 114
  and Arabs, 107–8
  equality and honour, 48
  Great Dissent, 6
  regulations, 102
  unification of humankind, 92–4, 99–100
Islamist movements, 7
Ismail, 100

Al-Jabarti, Abdelrahman, 4
Al-Jabbar, 88
jahiliyya, 39, 108
Janad, province of, 61–2
Jesus Christ, 40–1, 68, 82
Jews, 73
jihad, 30, 70–2, 95
Joseph, Prophet, 68
judges, 28, 37, 70
judicial authority, 59–64
jurisprudence, 21, 70

Kalilah wa Dimnah, 46
Khalafallah, Muhammad Ahmad, 13
Khalid, Khalid Muhammad, 13
Khalid ibn al-Walid, 61, 113
Khalid ibn Sai'd ibn al-'As, 72
Kharijites, 17, 35, 45, 52
Khawarij, 6
khums, 61
Khuza'i, Ali ibn Muhammad, 75

legislation, 73, 74, 77, 102
Liberal-Constitutionalist Party, 6, 7
Locke, John, 9, 34

Index

Maghrawah, 30
Maghrib, 30
Mamluks, 50, 55
Al-Mansur, Abu Ja'afar, 28n, 31, 32n
market inspectors, 70
mathematics, 46
Mawāqif, 38, 43
Mecca, 50n, 61, 103
Medina, 44n, 50, 103
Mehmet VI, Sultan of Turkey, 47
Messenger of God, 27, 28, 37, 50, 62–3, 65, 68–9, 72, 77, 81, 82, 83, 87, 89–92, 93, 100, 102, 103, 105n, 107, 110, 117
military commanders, 37, 64
monarchical caliphate, 1, 6, 12, 29–30, 55, 69
monarchy, 32, 34, 48, 50–1, 86, 116
Moses, 82, 105n
Mu'ad ibn Jabal, 60, 61–3, 72
Mu'awiya ibn Abi Sufyan, 29, 47, 49
muezzin, 70
mufti, 70
Al Mughira ibn Shu'ba, 62
Muhajirun and Ansar, 105, 109
Muhammad, Prophet, 79, 100
   'Ali and, 45n
   apostle of God, 87, 103–4
   appointment of judges, 28, 59–64, 101
   companions of, 1, 27n, 36, 37, 44, 60–1, 69, 105, 109, 118
   conversion by persuasion, 71
   death and end of prophetic mission, 43, 45n, 102, 104, 105–6, 107
   ideal of simplicity, 76–8
   jihad, 70–2

spiritual/temporal authority, 65, 67–9, 72–5, 81, 82, 83, 84–9, 92, 94–6, 101–3
succession, 104–6, 109–10, 111–12
Mu'izz al-Dawla, 55
Muslim Brotherhood, 7
Mu'ta, battle of, 71n
Al-Mutalmiss, 109–10
Al-Mu'tasim, 30
Al Mu'tassim Billah, 55
Al-Mutawakkil, 30
Mu'tazilah al-Asamm, 35
Mu'tazilites, 4, 9, 17, 44n, 52
Al-Muti'i, Muhammad Bakhit, *124*

Najm al-Din al-Ayyubi, 50
Naqfi, Tarih ibn Ismail, 32
nation-states, 15
nationalism, 2, 3, 6, 7
Al-Nazzam, 44
Nietzsche, Friedrich, 16
Nur-al-Din al-Halabi, 'Ali Ibn Ibrahim, 63

Ottoman Empire, 1–2, 7, 45n, 50, 51–2, 56
Oxford University, 8–9

Persia, 71
pilgrimage, 61, 62, 77, 110
Plato, 46
political institutions, 2, 8, 70
political modernisation, 3, 9
political science, 44–5, 46, 50–1, 118
polytheism, 41, 93, 108
prayers, 21, 48, 62, 63, 64, 70, 77
print press, 4
prophetic mission, 73, 74, 82–5, 89, 95–6, 100

Qabus ibn Mus'ab, 68
Qarmatis, 55
Al-Qayrawan, 30
Al-Qazwini, Najm al-Din, 32, 33
Qur'an, 22, 27, 53–4, 61, 77
  on the Arabs, 102–3
  and the caliphate, 36–8, 39, 52
  on fasting, 78
  on God's messenger, 83, 89–92, 103
  inner meaning of, 45n
  on spiritual and temporal power, 87–9, 95
  teaching of, 70
  and unification of humankind, 93
Qurayshi, 39, 92, 100, 113, 115

Rafidites, 44n
Al-Rashid, 29
rationality, 4–5, 9, 10, 11, 35
Raymond, André, 3–4
Rayyan ibn al Walid, Pharaoh of Egypt, 68
Razek, Mustafa, 8
Al-Rāzī Qutb al-Din, 33
rebellion, 41, 116
religious controversy, 5–7, 12–14
religious conversion, 61, 70–2, 88
Rida, Rashid, 9, 38–9, *125*
Rifa'a Al Tahtāwī, 64, 69–70, 75

Sa'd ibn 'Ubadah, 110, 113
Saif al-Dawla, 55
scholarship, 14–15
science, 4, 44, 75
secularism, 3, 5, 8, 14, 85, 94, 107
Seljuks, 56
sharī'a, 25, 28–9, 35, 40, 41
Shawqi, Ahmad, 95n
Shi'a, 6, 17, 44n, 45n, 104

Al-Sialakuti, Abd al-Hakim, 33
Al-Siddiq *see* Abu Bakr
Sinhajah, 30
slavery, 41
social sciences, 5, 9, 118
sociology, 14
Soroush, Abdolkarim, 15
sovereignty, 3, 27, 33–4, 49, 85, 87, 96
Spain, 30
Spinoza, Baruch, 16
Sufis, 45n
sunna, 38, 39, 92, 95, 104–5
Sunni Muslims, 6, 8, 10, 12, 16–17, 45n, 104n
superstition, 11
Syria, 52
Syrian Christians, 50n

Al-Tabari, Muhammad ibn Jarir, 72, 105n
Al-Taftazai, Mas'ud ibn 'Amr ibn 'Abdallah, 39, *124*
Taha, Mahmood Muhammad, 15
Taif, 103
Tamim tribe, 113
Tartars, 55
Al-Tirmidhi, 60, 62
translators, 44, 70
Turkish Grand National Assembly, 334

'Ubaydid (Fatimids), 30
'ulamā, 2–3, 8, 14, 32
'Umar ibn al-Khattab, 33, 60, 105, 114
Umayyads, 1, 29, 30, 32n, 49n, 50, 51
umma, 1, 2, 6, 28, 33–4, 45n, 46, 51, 86, 101

Wafd Party, 3, 6, 7
Al-Walid, Khalid ibn, 61, 113

Index

Al-Walid ibn Yazid, 32
Wasit, 55
Wittgenstein, Ludwig, 16

Ya'la ibn Abi Umayya, 72
Yazid ibn al-Muqaffa', 49n
Yazid ibn Mu'awiyya, 49n, 50, 51
Yemen, 55, 60–1, 62, 63, 72

Zaher Bibars, 55
Al-Zahiri, Daoud ibn Khalaf, 44n
Zahirites, 44n, 105
zakat, 62, 63, 72, 113
Al-Zamakhshari, 26n, 108n, *124*
Zanatah rulers, 30
Zaydis, 44n

EU Authorised Representative:
Easy Access System Europe Mustamäe tee 50, 10621 Tallinn, Estonia
gpsr.requests@easproject.com

Printed and bound by CPI Group (UK) Ltd, Croydon, CR0 4YY
02/03/2026
02063695-0001